75 CLASSIC
RISOTTO
RECIPES

75 CLASSIC
RISOTTO
RECIPES

deliciously authentic dishes made easy
in over 280 step-by-step photographs

how to cook rice and risotto to perfection with tempting ideas for
all occasions, from simple suppers to dinner-party showstoppers

CHRISTINE INGRAM

southwater

This edition is published by Southwater, an imprint of Anness Publishing Ltd,
Hermes House, 88–89 Blackfriars Road, London SE1 8HA; tel. 020 7401 2077; fax 020 7633 9499

www.southwaterbooks.com; www.annesspublishing.com

If you like the images in this book and would like to investigate using them for publishing, promotions or advertising,
please visit our website www.practicalpictures.com for more information.

UK distributor: Book Trade Services; tel. 0116 2759086; fax 0116 2759090; uksales@booktradeservices.com;
exportsales@booktradeservices.com
North American distributor: National Book Network; tel. 301 459 3366; fax 301 429 5746; www.nbnbooks.com
Australian distributor: Pan Macmillan Australia; tel. 1300 135 113; fax 1300 135 103; customer.service@macmillan.com.au
New Zealand distributor: David Bateman Ltd; tel. (09) 415 7664; fax (09) 415 8892

Publisher: Joanna Lorenz
Project Editor: Sarah Ainley
Copy Editor: Jenni Fleetwood
Designer: Penny Dawes
Photography: Dave King (recipes) and David Jordan (cutouts and techniques)
Food for Photography: Jennie Shapter (recipes) and Sara Lewis (cutouts and techniques)
Stylist: Jo Harris
Recipes: Carla Capalbo, Kit Chan, Roz Denny, Rafi Fernandez, Silvana Franco, Deh-Ta Hsiung, Shehzad Husain,
Christine Ingram, Soheila Kimberley, Masaki Ko, Elizabeth Lambert Ortiz, Ruby Le Bois and Sallie Morris
Production Controller: Christine Ni

ETHICAL TRADING POLICY

Because of our ongoing ecological investment programme, you, as our customer, can have the pleasure and reassurance
of knowing that a tree is being cultivated on your behalf to naturally replace the materials used to make the book
you are holding. For further information about this scheme, go to www.annesspublishing.com/trees

Previously published as *Risotto*

NOTES

For all recipes, quantities are given in both metric
and imperial measures and, where appropriate,
in standard cups and spoons. Follow one set
of measures, but not a mixture, because they
are not interchangeable.
Standard spoon and cup measures are level.
1 tsp = 5ml, 1 tbsp = 15ml, 1 cup = 250ml/8fl oz.
Australian standard tablespoons are 20ml. Australian
readers should use 3 tsp in place of 1 tbsp for
measuring small quantities.

American pints are 16fl oz/2 cups. American
readers should use 20fl oz/2.5 cups in place
of 1 pint when measuring liquids.
Electric oven temperatures in this book are for
conventional ovens. When using a fan oven, the
temperature will probably need to be reduced by
about 10–20°C/20–40°F. Since ovens vary, you
should check with your manufacturer's instruction
book for guidance.
Medium (US large) eggs are used unless
otherwise stated.

Main front cover image shows Risotto with Asparagus – for recipe, see page 30.

PUBLISHER'S NOTE

Although the advice and information in this book are believed to be accurate and true at the time of going to press, neither the authors
nor the publisher can accept any legal responsibility or liability for any errors or omissions that may have been made nor for any
inaccuracies nor for any loss, harm or injury that comes about from following instructions or advice in this book.

CONTENTS

INTRODUCTION

Risotto: the word sounds rich and sensuous, which is just how this delicious Italian dish should be. First comes the aroma — redolent of wine, good stock and simple herbs. Then the texture — plump grains of rice cooked until creamy and tender, with just a hint of firmness at the centre. Finally, the flavour — whatever ingredients you add, this style of cooking blends the flavours beautifully. Best of all, risotto is a simple dish to cook. It does require your undivided attention, but only for a half hour of gentle stirring, while the grains gradually cook to perfection.

THE HISTORY OF RISOTTO

This simple Italian dish is very much a peasant food and it says a great deal about the changing attitudes towards food and healthy eating that in the last decade or so, this dish, like much of *cucina povera*, has come to be so widely appreciated. Nowadays you will see risotto on the menu at some of the classiest restaurants in town, enjoyed for the same reasons it has always been valued, because it is healthy, satisfying and extremely good to eat. Yet what could be simpler than a risotto? Although there are complicated and elaborate versions, some of the best risottos are made using little more than rice, a good stock and a few fresh herbs or cheeses. These simple risottos, like *Risi e Bisi* (Rice and Peas) or *Risotto alla Parmigiana* (Rice with Cheese) are probably the most traditional of all, and are no less tasty for their plain ingredients.

Since the first risottos were the food of poorer people, there is no long line of recipes that chart the popularity of this dish. Recipe books written in Italy during risotto's infancy tended to concern themselves with costly meats or spices and were written for the wealthy who could afford these expensive ingredients. Peasants and poor farmers had neither the time, the ability nor the inclination to read what they knew already: that rice was a cheap and sustaining food that was also delicious when cooked with care.

Short grain rice, which is the central ingredient in risotto, has been grown in Italy for several hundred years. The Arabs introduced rice into Italy during the Middle Ages, but this early rice was a longer grained variety and was grown in Sicily and the south of the country.

At some point though, rice was introduced to Lombardy in northern Italy, and by the 15th century, rice cultivation had become an established part of the Italian way of life. It was around this time that the custom of cultivating rice in fields flooded with water was adopted in Italy; this method of growing rice followed the process used in Asia, as opposed to the method of dry cultivation favoured by the Arabs.

Today, Italy shares with Spain the honour of being Europe's leading rice producer. Risotto rices are still grown in the north of the country, where the rice fields are irrigated with water running down from the Alps. The varieties of rice grown today have been improved and refined since earlier times, yet the characteristic starchy short grain has remained the same.

The method of cooking rice in stock may have been influenced by cooking styles in France and Spain but, whether by accident or design, it is difficult to imagine a better way of doing justice to fine rice than to serve it as a risotto.

Risotto is traditionally eaten as a separate course before the meat and vegetables. Only rice and stock are the essential ingredients, but you should choose these carefully. The stock must be home-made (or the very best you can afford) and the rice must be one of those recommended for the purpose. Have the stock simmering in a pan adjacent to the risotto pan, and add it slowly and lovingly. Observe the standing time at the end, as this allows the rice to rest and reach perfection. Do all this – and it is not difficult – and you'll find risotto one of the most simple and rewarding rice dishes you can make.

Types of Risotto Rice

It is essential to use a risotto rice, but precisely which one is up to you. Named risotto rices are becoming more widely available, but you will often find packages labelled simply Italian risotto rice. Of the named varieties, Arborio is the most widely available, with Carnaroli and Vialone Nano becoming increasingly easy to find in Italian delicatessens and good supermarkets. Other specific types of risotto rice include Baldo, Vialone Nano Gigante and Roma. Each has its own particular qualities, which will be familiar to those who specialize in cooking *risotti*. Some recipes call for a named risotto rice, but most are non-specific and any risotto rice will give a good result.

INSTANT RISOTTOS

There are several instant risottos on the market, available from supermarkets and delicatessens. They are easy to make: all you need to do is add water, heat and stir. Packets give simple instructions and recommend simmering for about 10 minutes – roughly half the time required for making a classic risotto. Instant risottos come in several flavours, including four cheeses, spinach, saffron, tomato and black cuttlefish. They are handy for a quick meal, and the colours supplied by the flavourings make them pretty to serve. More importantly, these risottos taste surprisingly good.

Left: Clockwise from top, instant risottos flavoured with cuttlefish, tomatoes, saffron and spinach.

COOKING PERFECT RISOTTO

1 In a large, deep saucepan, fry the onion, garlic and any other vegetable(s) in extra virgin olive oil over a medium heat for a few minutes, stirring all the time. Unless the recipe specifies otherwise, the onion and other vegetables should be softened but not browned.

2 If using any uncooked meat or poultry, add these ingredients to the onions in the pan, unless the recipe specifies otherwise. Turn up the heat to high and cook, stirring frequently, until browned on all sides.

3 Tip the risotto rice into the pan, and stir, so that every grain is coated in the oil. Fry the rice over a high heat for 3–4 minutes, stirring all the time. You will notice that the grains of rice become transparent as they are stirred into the hot oil, except for the very centre of the grain, which remains opaque.

4 Add a little wine, if this is what is called for in the recipe, or a ladleful of hot stock. Stir the rice until all the liquid has been absorbed.

5 Lower the heat to moderate, then add another ladleful of hot stock and stir it into the rice. Keep the pan over a moderate heat so that the liquid bubbles but the rice is in no danger of burning. Stir the rice frequently.

6 Add the remaining stock a ladleful at a time, making sure that each ladleful is used up before adding the next. This process will take about 20 minutes. As the risotto cooks, the grains of rice will begin to soften and merge together.

7 When the risotto begins to look creamy, grate in the cheese or add extra butter. The rice should be virtually tender, but still a little hard in the centre. At this point remove the pan from the heat, cover with a dish towel and leave to rest for about 5 minutes. The risotto will cook to perfection in the residual heat.

RISOTTO TIPS
• To begin, fry the rice in hot oil, stirring all the time, until the grains are coated and begin to turn translucent.
• Add any wine or sherry to the risotto before adding the stock. The alcohol will evaporate, but the flavour will remain.
• Use a good quality, home-made stock for your risotto. Alternatively, buy cartons of fresh stock, which are available from delicatessens and large supermarkets.
• The stock added to a risotto must always be hot. Have it simmering in a separate pan adjacent to the pan in which you are cooking the risotto.
• Add the hot stock slowly, ladleful by ladleful. Make sure all the liquid has been absorbed before adding the next ladleful.
• Avoid overcooking the risotto. Remove the pan from the heat while the rice is still slightly undercooked.
• For best results, season the risotto after cooking but before leaving it to rest. Stock, salted butter and Parmesan cheese will all contribute some saltiness, as may other ingredients, so always taste the risotto before adding any extra salt.
• Don't use ready-grated Parmesan. For the best flavour, buy good quality Parmesan in one piece and grate it yourself.

Equipment

There are only three essential pieces of equipment needed for cooking a risotto, and with luck you'll have them already.
• A heavy-based pan. Ideally, this should be a wide, straight-sided pot, deep enough to contain the cooked risotto. A deep frying pan can be used for smaller quantities.
• A wooden spoon.
• A saucepan for the simmering stock.

ADDING RISOTTO INGREDIENTS

Recipes will tell you when to stir in any additional ingredients needed for the risotto, but this guide may be helpful when devising your own risotto recipes.

Vegetables Onions and garlic are fried until soft at the beginning, before the rice is added. Most other vegetables, such as aubergines, carrots, courgettes and pepper, are sautéed with the onions. Vegetables that require little cooking, such as spinach and asparagus, should be stirred in towards the end of cooking. Mushrooms are usually fried at the same time or just after the onions, before adding the rice.

Above: Onions and garlic are essential ingredients in a good risotto. Use red onions or shallots for variations in flavour.

Above: Fresh green vegetables, such as courgettes, spinach and asparagus, add texture to the risotto. They retain their shape and colour during cooking, and always look impressive.

Fish and shellfish These are generally cooked before being added to the risotto. It is usual for fillets of fish, such as salmon, plaice or sea bass to be poached, then flaked. Scallops should be lightly cooked, then sliced. Stir fish or shellfish into the risotto about three-quarters of the way through cooking.

Above: Almost any fresh fish and seafood can be used in a risotto, including salmon fillets, haddock, plaice and tiger prawns.

Meat and poultry These are usually added at an early stage, at the same time as the onions; the rice is added later, so that both ingredients cook together. The exception is cooked meats, such as sausage or ham, which tend to be stirred into the risotto towards the end of cooking.

Above: Chicken fillets and gammon are both very successful ingredients for risottos, but the choice really is endless. Cut the meat into small pieces and brown with the onions before stirring in the rice.

Herbs Robust herbs are sometimes cooked with the onions, but more delicate herbs, such as parsley or coriander, are usually added at the end of cooking, at the same time as the Parmesan cheese or butter.

Above: Delicate-flavoured herbs, such as thyme, sage, coriander and tarragon, can all be stirred into the cooked rice for a simple risotto.

Cheese Where cheese is the dominant flavouring, as in a four-cheese risotto, it can be added halfway through cooking, but it is more usual for grated Parmesan to be added just before the risotto is left to rest.

Above: Most cheeses can be used in risottos but the one essential cheese is Parmesan. Use it either on its own as a simple flavouring or to complement other ingredients in the recipe. Fresh shavings of Parmesan can be used to garnish the risotto, or supply a bowl of Parmesan, grated fresh from the block, to be passed separately when serving.

MAKING STOCKS

Chicken Stock

MAKES ABOUT 1.5 LITRES/2½ PINTS/6¼ CUPS

INGREDIENTS
1 onion, quartered
2 celery sticks, chopped
1 carrot, roughly chopped
about 675g/1½lb fresh chicken,
  either ½ whole chicken or 2–3
  chicken quarters
1 fresh thyme or marjoram sprig
2 fresh parsley sprigs
8 whole peppercorns
salt

1 Put the prepared vegetables in a large, heavy-based saucepan and lay the chicken on top. Pour over cold water to cover the chicken (about 1.5 litres/2½ pints/6¼ cups).

2 Bring to the boil slowly. Do not cover the pan. When bubbling, skim off any fat that has risen to the surface.

3 Add the herbs, peppercorns and a pinch of salt. Lower the heat, cover the pan and simmer the stock gently for 2–2½ hours, until the chicken is tender.

4 Using a slotted spoon, transfer the chicken or chicken pieces to a plate. Remove any skin or bones; the chicken can be used in another recipe. Strain the stock into a clean bowl, leave it to cool, then chill in the fridge.

5 A layer of fat will form on the surface of the chilled stock. Remove this just before use. The stock can be kept in the fridge for up to 3 days or frozen for up to 6 months.

Fish Stock

MAKES ABOUT 2.5 LITRES/4 PINTS/10 CUPS

INGREDIENTS
900g/2lb white fish bones and
  trimmings, but not gills
2.5 litres/4 pints/10 cups water
1 onion, roughly chopped
1 celery stick, chopped
1 carrot, chopped
1 bay leaf
3 fresh parsley sprigs
6 peppercorns
5cm/2in piece of pared lemon rind
75ml/5 tbsp/⅓ cup dry white wine

1 Put the fish bones and fish heads in a large, heavy-based saucepan. Pour in the water.

2 Bring the liquid to the boil, using a spoon to skim off any scum that rises to the surface. Add the onion, celery, carrot, bay leaf, parsley, peppercorns, lemon rind and white wine.

3 Lower the heat, and cover the pan with the lid. Simmer the stock gently for 20–30 minutes, then leave to cool.

4 Strain the cooled stock through a muslin bag into a clean bowl. Keep the stock in the fridge for up to 2 days or freeze it for up to 3 months.

COOK'S TIP
Do not allow the fish stock to boil for a prolonged period or the bones will begin to disintegrate and the stock will acquire an unpleasant, bitter flavour.

Vegetable Stock

MAKES ABOUT 1.2 LITRES/2 PINTS/5 CUPS

INGREDIENTS
3–4 shallots, halved
2 celery sticks or 75g/3oz celeriac,
  chopped
2 carrots, roughly chopped
3 tomatoes, halved
3 fresh parsley stalks
1 fresh tarragon sprig
1 fresh marjoram or thyme sprig
2.5cm/1in piece of pared orange rind
6 peppercorns
2 allspice berries
1.5 litres/2½ pints/6¼ cups water

1 Put all the vegetables into a heavy-based saucepan. Add the fresh herbs, orange rind and spices. Pour in the water.

2 Bring the liquid to the boil, then lower the heat and simmer the stock gently for 30 minutes. Leave it to cool completely.

3 Strain the stock through a sieve into a large bowl, pressing out all the liquid from the vegetables using the back of a spoon. Store the cold stock in the fridge for up to 3 days or in the freezer for up to 6 months.

THE RECIPES

Risotto is not a single dish, but the starting point for many, from the simple marriage of rice with stock and Parmesan, to sophisticated combinations like bacon, baby courgettes and peppers, or pumpkin and pistachio nuts. Some of the more interesting risottos here are based on vegetables, but seafood stars in several, and there are some superb meat medleys, too; chocolate and champagne are some of the more unusual ingredients. This collection includes risotto rice balls, timballes and fish cakes, plus all-in-one dishes, including biryani, paella, pilau and jambalaya, cousins of the Italian risotto.

FRIED RICE BALLS STUFFED WITH MOZZARELLA

THESE DEEP-FRIED BALLS OF RISOTTO GO BY THE NAME OF SUPPLI AL TELEFONO IN THEIR NATIVE ITALY. STUFFED WITH MOZZARELLA CHEESE, THEY ARE VERY POPULAR SNACKS, WHICH IS HARDLY SURPRISING AS THEY ARE QUITE DELICIOUS.

SERVES FOUR

INGREDIENTS

1 quantity Risotto with Parmesan or
  Mushroom Risotto
3 eggs
breadcrumbs and plain flour, to coat
115g/4oz/⅔ cup mozzarella cheese,
  cut into small cubes
oil, for deep-frying
dressed curly endive and cherry
  tomatoes, to serve

1 Put the risotto in a bowl and allow it to cool completely. Beat two of the eggs, and stir them into the cold risotto until well mixed.

2 Use your hands to form the rice mixture into balls the size of a large egg. If the mixture is too moist to hold its shape well, stir in a few tablespoons of breadcrumbs. Poke a hole into the centre of each ball with your finger, then fill it with a few small cubes of mozzarella, and close the hole over again with the rice mixture.

3 Heat the oil for deep-frying until a small piece of bread sizzles as soon as it is dropped in.

4 Spread some flour on a plate. Beat the remaining egg in a shallow bowl. Sprinkle another plate with breadcrumbs. Roll the balls in the flour, then in the egg, and finally in the breadcrumbs.

5 Fry them a few at a time in the hot oil until golden and crisp. Drain on kitchen paper while the remaining balls are being fried. Serve hot, with a simple salad of dressed curly endive leaves and cherry tomatoes.

COOK'S TIP
These provide the perfect solution as to what to do with leftover risotto, as they are best made with a cold mixture, cooked the day before.

SPINACH AND RICE SOUP

USE VERY YOUNG SPINACH LEAVES TO PREPARE THIS LIGHT AND FRESH-TASTING SOUP.

SERVES FOUR

INGREDIENTS
675g/1½lb fresh spinach leaves, washed
45ml/3 tbsp extra virgin olive oil
1 small onion, finely chopped
2 garlic cloves, finely chopped
1 small fresh red chilli, seeded and finely chopped
225g/8oz/generous 1 cup risotto rice
1.2 litres/2 pints/5 cups vegetable stock
salt and freshly ground black pepper
shavings of pared Parmesan or Pecorino cheese, to serve

1 Place the spinach in a large pan with just the water that clings to its leaves after washing. Add a large pinch of salt. Heat gently until the spinach has wilted, then remove from the heat and drain, reserving any liquid.

2 Either chop the spinach finely using a large kitchen knife or place in a food processor and process the leaves to a fairly coarse purée.

COOK'S TIP
Buy Parmesan or Pecorino cheese in the piece from a reputable supplier, and it will be full of flavour and easy to grate or shave with a vegetable peeler.

3 Heat the oil in a large saucepan and gently cook the onion, garlic and chilli for 4–5 minutes until softened. Stir in the rice until well coated, then pour in the stock and reserved spinach liquid. Bring to the boil, lower the heat and simmer for 10 minutes.

4 Add the spinach, with salt and pepper to taste. Cook for 5–7 minutes, until the rice is tender. Check the seasoning. Serve in heated bowls, topped with the shavings of cheese.

RISOTTO-STUFFED AUBERGINES WITH SPICY TOMATO SAUCE

AUBERGINES ARE A CHALLENGE TO THE CREATIVE COOK AND ALLOW FOR SOME UNUSUAL RECIPE IDEAS. HERE, THEY ARE FILLED WITH A RICE STUFFING AND BAKED WITH A CHEESE AND PINE NUT TOPPING.

SERVES FOUR

INGREDIENTS
  4 small aubergines
  105ml/7 tbsp olive oil
  1 small onion, chopped
  175g/6oz/scant 1 cup risotto rice
  750ml/1¼ pints/3 cups hot vegetable
    stock
  15ml/1 tbsp white wine vinegar
  25g/1oz/⅓ cup freshly grated
    Parmesan cheese
  15g/½oz/2 tbsp pine nuts
For the tomato sauce
  300ml/½ pint/1¼ cups thick passata
    or puréed tomatoes
  5ml/1 tsp mild curry paste
  pinch of salt

1 Preheat the oven to 200°C/400°F/
Gas 6. Cut the aubergines in half
lengthways, and remove the flesh with
a small knife. Brush the shells with
30ml/2 tbsp of the oil and bake on a
baking sheet, supported by crumpled
foil, for 6–8 minutes.

2 Chop the aubergine flesh. Heat the
remaining oil in a medium pan. Add
the aubergine flesh and the onion, and
cook over a gentle heat for 3–4 minutes
until soft. Add the rice and stock, and
leave to simmer, uncovered, for about
15 minutes. Add the vinegar.

COOK'S TIP
If the aubergine shells do not stand
level, cut a thin slice from the bottom.

3 Increase the oven temperature to
230°C/450°F/Gas 8. Spoon the rice
mixture into the aubergine skins, top
with the cheese and pine nuts, return
to the oven and brown for 5 minutes.

4 To make the sauce, mix the passata
or puréed tomatoes with the curry paste
in a small pan. Heat through and add
salt to taste. Spoon the sauce on to four
individual serving plates and arrange
two aubergine halves on each one.

RICE CAKES WITH SMOKED SALMON

These elegant rice cakes are made using a risotto base. You could skip this stage and use leftover Seafood or Mushroom Risotto. Alternatively, use leftover long grain rice and add extra flavour with spring onions.

SERVES FOUR

INGREDIENTS

30ml/2 tbsp olive oil
1 medium onion, chopped
225g/8oz/generous 1 cup risotto rice
about 90ml/6 tbsp white wine
about 750ml/1¼ pints/3 cups fish or
  chicken stock
15g/½oz/2 tbsp dried porcini
  mushrooms, soaked for 10 minutes
  in warm water to cover
15ml/1 tbsp chopped fresh parsley
15ml/1 tbsp snipped fresh chives
5ml/1 tsp chopped fresh dill
1 egg, lightly beaten
about 45ml/3 tbsp ground rice, plus
  extra for dusting
oil, for frying
60ml/4 tbsp soured cream
175g/6oz smoked salmon
salt and freshly ground black pepper
radicchio and oakleaf salad, tossed
  in French dressing, to serve

1 Heat the olive oil in a pan and fry the onion for 3–4 minutes until soft. Add the rice and cook, stirring, until the grains are thoroughly coated in oil. Pour in the wine and stock, a little at a time, stirring constantly over a gentle heat until each quantity of liquid has been absorbed before adding more.

2 Drain the mushrooms and chop them into small pieces. When the rice is tender, and all the liquid has been absorbed, stir in the mushrooms, parsley, chives, dill and seasoning. Remove from the heat and set aside for a few minutes to cool.

COOK'S TIP
For a sophisticated occasion, garnish the rice cakes with roasted baby asparagus spears, lemon slices and dill.

3 Add the beaten egg, then stir in enough ground rice to bind the mixture – it should be soft but manageable. Dust your hands with ground rice and shape the mixture into four patties, about 13cm/5in in diameter and about 2cm/¾in thick.

4 Heat the oil in a shallow pan and fry the rice cakes, in batches if necessary, for 4–5 minutes until evenly browned on both sides. Drain on kitchen paper and cool slightly. Place each rice cake on a plate and top with 15ml/1 tbsp soured cream. Twist two or three thin slices of smoked salmon on top, and serve with a dressed salad garnish.

TROUT <u>AND</u> PARMA HAM RISOTTO ROLLS

THIS MAKES A DELICIOUS AND ELEGANT MEAL. THE RISOTTO — MADE WITH PORCINI MUSHROOMS AND PRAWNS — IS A FINE MATCH FOR THE ROBUST FLAVOUR OF THE TROUT ROLLS.

<u>SERVES FOUR</u>

INGREDIENTS
 4 trout fillets, skinned
 4 slices Parma ham
 caper berries, to garnish
For the risotto
 30ml/2 tbsp olive oil
 8 large raw prawns, peeled and
  deveined
 1 medium onion, chopped
 225g/8oz/generous 1 cup risotto
  rice
 about 105ml/7 tbsp white wine
 about 750ml/1¼ pints/3 cups
  simmering fish or chicken stock
 15g/½oz/2 tbsp dried porcini or
  chanterelle mushrooms, soaked
  for 10 minutes in warm water to
  cover
 salt and freshly ground black pepper

2 Add the chopped onion to the oil remaining in the pan and fry over a gentle heat for 3–4 minutes until soft. Add the rice and stir for 3–4 minutes until the grains are evenly coated in oil. Add 75ml/5 tbsp of the wine and then the stock, a little at a time, stirring over a gentle heat and allowing the rice to absorb the liquid before adding more.

4 Remove the pan from the heat and stir in the prawns. Preheat the oven to 190ºC/375ºF/Gas 5.

5 Take a trout fillet, place a spoonful of risotto at one end and roll up. Wrap each fillet in a slice of Parma ham and place in a greased ovenproof dish.

1 First make the risotto. Heat the oil in a heavy-based saucepan or deep frying pan and fry the prawns very briefly until flecked with pink. Lift out on a slotted spoon and transfer to a plate.

3 Drain the mushrooms, reserving the liquid, and cut the larger ones in half. Towards the end of cooking, stir the mushrooms into the risotto with 15ml/ 1 tbsp of the reserved mushroom liquid. If the rice is not yet *al dente*, add a little more stock or mushroom liquid and cook for 2–3 minutes more. Season to taste with salt and pepper.

6 Spoon any remaining risotto around the fish fillets and sprinkle over the rest of the wine. Cover loosely with foil and bake for 15–20 minutes until the fish is tender. Spoon the risotto on to a platter, top with the trout rolls and garnish with caper berries. Serve at once.

COOK'S TIP
There are no hard and fast rules about which type of risotto to use for this dish. Almost any risotto recipe could be used, although a vegetable or seafood risotto would be particularly suitable.

STUFFED CHICKEN ROLLS

THESE DELICIOUS CHICKEN ROLLS ARE SIMPLE TO MAKE, BUT SOPHISTICATED ENOUGH TO SERVE AT A DINNER PARTY, ESPECIALLY IF YOU ARRANGE SLICES ON A BED OF TAGLIATELLE TOSSED WITH FRIED WILD MUSHROOMS.

SERVES FOUR

INGREDIENTS

   25g/1oz/2 tbsp butter
   1 garlic clove, chopped
   150g/5oz/1¼ cups cooked risotto rice
   45ml/3 tbsp ricotta cheese
   10ml/2 tsp chopped fresh flat leaf
    parsley
   5ml/1 tsp chopped fresh tarragon
   4 skinless, boneless chicken breasts
   3–4 slices Parma ham
   15ml/1 tbsp olive oil
   120ml/4fl oz/½ cup white wine
   salt and freshly ground black pepper
   fresh flat leaf parsley sprigs, to
    garnish
   cooked tagliatelle and sautéed
    blewit mushrooms, to serve
    (optional)

1 Preheat the oven to 180°C/350°F/ Gas 4. Melt about 10g/¼oz/2 tsp of the butter in a small pan and fry the garlic for a few seconds without browning. Spoon into a bowl.

COOK'S TIP
White long grain rice could be used in place of risotto rice in this dish. Long grain rice has a different consistency to risotto rice, and will make a less dense stuffing for the chicken rolls.

2 Add the rice, ricotta, parsley and tarragon and season with salt and pepper. Stir to mix.

3 Place each chicken breast in turn between two sheets of clear film and flatten by beating lightly, but firmly, with a rolling pin.

4 Divide the slices of Parma ham between the chicken breasts, trimming the ham to fit, if necessary.

5 Place a spoonful of the rice stuffing at the wider end of each ham-topped breast. Roll up carefully and tie in place with cooking string or secure with a cocktail stick.

6 Heat the oil and the remaining butter in a frying pan and lightly fry the chicken rolls until browned on all sides. Place side by side in a shallow baking dish and pour over the white wine.

7 Cover the dish with greaseproof paper and cook in the oven for 30–35 minutes until the chicken is tender.

8 Cut the rolls into slices and serve on a bed of tagliatelle with sautéed blewit mushrooms and a generous grinding of black pepper, if you like. Garnish with sprigs of flat leaf parsley.

PUMPKIN AND PISTACHIO RISOTTO

VEGETARIANS TIRED OF THE STANDARD DINNER PARTY FARE WILL LOVE THIS ELEGANT COMBINATION OF CREAMY, GOLDEN RICE AND ORANGE PUMPKIN, AND SO WILL EVERYONE ELSE. IT WOULD LOOK PARTICULARLY IMPRESSIVE SERVED IN THE HOLLOWED-OUT PUMPKIN SHELL.

SERVES FOUR

INGREDIENTS
  1.2 litres/2 pints/5 cups vegetable
    stock or water
  generous pinch of saffron strands
  30ml/2 tbsp olive oil
  1 onion, chopped
  2 garlic cloves, crushed
  900g/2lb pumpkin, peeled, seeded
    and cut into 2cm/¾in cubes (about
    7 cups)
  400g/14oz/2 cups risotto rice
  200ml/7fl oz/scant 1 cup dry white
    wine
  30ml/2 tbsp freshly grated Parmesan
    cheese
  50g/2oz/½ cup pistachios, coarsely
    chopped
  45ml/3 tbsp chopped fresh marjoram
    or oregano, plus leaves to garnish
  salt, freshly grated nutmeg and
    freshly ground black pepper

1 Bring the stock or water to the boil and reduce to a low simmer. Ladle a little of it into a small bowl. Add the saffron strands and leave to infuse.

2 Heat the oil in a large, heavy-based saucepan or deep frying pan. Add the onion and garlic and cook gently for about 5 minutes until softened. Add the pumpkin and rice and stir to coat everything in oil. Cook for a few more minutes until the rice looks transparent.

3 Pour in the wine and allow it to bubble hard. When it has been absorbed, add a quarter of the hot stock or water and the saffron liquid. Stir until all the liquid has been absorbed. Gradually add the remaining stock or water, a little at a time, allowing the rice to absorb the liquid before adding more, and stirring constantly. After 20–30 minutes the rice should be golden yellow, creamy and *al dente*.

4 Stir in the Parmesan cheese, cover the pan and leave the risotto to stand for 5 minutes. To finish, stir in the pistachios and marjoram or oregano. Season to taste with a little salt, nutmeg and pepper, scatter over a few marjoram or oregano leaves and serve.

RISOTTO WITH PARMESAN

THIS TRADITIONAL RISOTTO IS SIMPLY FLAVOURED WITH GRATED PARMESAN CHEESE AND GOLDEN, FRIED CHOPPED ONION.

SERVES THREE TO FOUR

INGREDIENTS
1 litre/1¾ pints/4 cups beef,
  chicken or vegetable stock
65g/2½oz/5 tbsp butter
1 small onion, finely chopped
275g/10oz/1½ cups risotto rice
120ml/4fl oz/½ cup dry white wine
75g/3oz/1 cup freshly grated Parmesan
  cheese, plus extra to garnish
basil leaves, to garnish
salt and freshly ground black pepper

1 Heat the stock in a saucepan, and leave to simmer until needed.

2 Melt two-thirds of the butter in a large heavy-based saucepan or deep frying pan. Stir in the onion, and cook gently until soft and golden.

3 Add the rice and stir to coat the grains with butter. After 1–2 minutes, pour in the white wine. Raise the heat slightly, and cook until the wine evaporates. Add one small ladleful of the hot stock. Cook until the stock has been absorbed, stirring constantly.

4 Gradually add the remaining stock, a little at a time, allowing the rice to absorb the liquid before adding more, and stirring constantly. After 20–30 minutes the rice should be creamy and *al dente*. Season to taste.

5 Remove the pan from the heat. Stir in the remaining butter and the Parmesan cheese. Taste again for seasoning. Allow the risotto to rest for 3–4 minutes before serving, garnished with basil leaves and shavings of Parmesan, if you like.

COOK'S TIP
If you run out of stock when cooking the risotto, use hot water, but do not worry if the rice is done before you have used up all the stock.

RISOTTO WITH RICOTTA AND BASIL

THIS IS A WELL-FLAVOURED RISOTTO, WHICH BENEFITS FROM THE DISTINCT PUNGENCY OF BASIL, MELLOWED WITH SMOOTH RICOTTA.

SERVES THREE TO FOUR

INGREDIENTS
    45ml/3 tbsp olive oil
    1 onion, finely chopped
    275g/10oz/1½ cups risotto rice
    1 litre/1¾ pints/4 cups hot chicken
      or vegetable stock
    175g/6oz/¾ cup ricotta cheese
    50g/2oz/generous 1 cup fresh basil
      leaves, finely chopped, plus extra
      to garnish
    75g/3oz/1 cup freshly grated
      Parmesan cheese
    salt and freshly ground black pepper

1 Heat the oil in a large saucepan or flameproof casserole and fry the onion over a gentle heat until soft.

2 Tip in the rice. Cook for a few minutes, stirring, until the rice is coated with oil and is slightly translucent.

3 Pour in about a quarter of the stock. Cook, stirring, until all the stock has been absorbed, then add another ladleful. Continue in this manner, adding more stock when the previous ladleful has been absorbed, until the risotto has been cooking for about 20 minutes and the rice is just tender.

4 Spoon the ricotta into a bowl and break it up a little with a fork. Stir into the risotto along with the basil and Parmesan. Taste and adjust the seasoning, then cover and let stand for 2–3 minutes before serving, garnished with basil leaves.

RISOTTO FRITTATA

*HALF OMELETTE, HALF RISOTTO, THIS MAKES A DELIGHTFUL LIGHT LUNCH OR SUPPER DISH.
IF POSSIBLE, COOK EACH FRITTATA SEPARATELY, AND PREFERABLY IN A SMALL, CAST IRON PAN,
SO THAT THE EGGS COOK QUICKLY UNDERNEATH BUT STAY MOIST ON TOP.*

SERVES FOUR

INGREDIENTS

30–45ml/2–3 tbsp olive oil
1 small onion, finely chopped
1 garlic clove, crushed
1 large red pepper, seeded and cut
   into thin strips
150g/5oz/¾ cup risotto rice
400–475ml/14–16fl oz/1⅔–2 cups
   simmering chicken stock
25–40g/1–1½oz/2–3 tbsp butter
175g/6oz/2½ cups button
   mushrooms, finely sliced
60ml/4 tbsp freshly grated Parmesan
   cheese
6–8 eggs
salt and freshly ground black pepper

1 Heat 15ml/1 tbsp oil in a large frying pan and fry the onion and garlic over a gentle heat for 2–3 minutes until the onion begins to soften but does not brown. Add the pepper and cook, stirring, for 4–5 minutes, until soft.

2 Stir in the rice and cook gently for 2–3 minutes, stirring all the time, until the grains are evenly coated with oil.

3 Add a quarter of the chicken stock and season. Stir over a low heat until the stock has been absorbed. Continue to add more stock, a little at a time, allowing the rice to absorb the liquid before adding more. Continue cooking in this way until the rice is *al dente*.

4 In a separate small pan, heat a little of the remaining oil and some butter and quickly fry the mushrooms until golden. Transfer to a plate.

5 When the rice is tender, remove from the heat and stir in the mushrooms and Parmesan cheese.

6 Beat together the eggs with 40ml/ 8 tsp cold water and season well. Heat the remaining oil and butter in an omelette pan and add the risotto mixture. Spread the mixture out in the pan, then immediately add the beaten egg, tilting the pan so that the omelette cooks evenly. Fry over a moderately high heat for 1–2 minutes, then transfer to a warmed plate and serve.

COOK'S TIP
This will make a more substantial dish for two, using five or six eggs. If preferred, the frittata could be cooked as individual portions.

PORCINI AND PARMESAN RISOTTO

THE SUCCESS OF A GOOD RISOTTO DEPENDS ON BOTH THE QUALITY OF THE RICE USED AND THE TECHNIQUE. ADD THE STOCK GRADUALLY AND STIR CONSTANTLY TO COAX A CREAMY TEXTURE FROM THE STARCH GRAINS. THIS VARIATION ON THE CLASSIC RISOTTO ALLA MILANESE INCLUDES SAFFRON, PORCINI MUSHROOMS AND PARMESAN.

SERVES FOUR

INGREDIENTS
15g/½oz/2 tbsp dried porcini
  mushrooms
150ml/¼ pint/⅔ cup warm water
1 litre/1¾ pints/4 cups vegetable stock
generous pinch of saffron strands
30ml/2 tbsp olive oil
1 onion, finely chopped
1 garlic clove, crushed
350g/12oz/1¾ cups Arborio or
  Carnaroli rice
150ml/¼ pint/⅔ cup dry white wine
25g/1oz/2 tbsp butter
50g/2oz/⅔ cup freshly grated
  Parmesan cheese
salt and freshly ground black pepper
pink and yellow oyster mushrooms,
  to serve (optional)

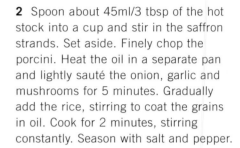

1 Put the dried porcini in a bowl and pour over the warm water. Leave the mushrooms to soak for 20 minutes, then lift out with a slotted spoon. Filter the soaking water through a layer of kitchen paper in a sieve, then place it in a saucepan with the stock. Bring the liquid to a gentle simmer.

2 Spoon about 45ml/3 tbsp of the hot stock into a cup and stir in the saffron strands. Set aside. Finely chop the porcini. Heat the oil in a separate pan and lightly sauté the onion, garlic and mushrooms for 5 minutes. Gradually add the rice, stirring to coat the grains in oil. Cook for 2 minutes, stirring constantly. Season with salt and pepper.

3 Pour in the white wine. Cook, stirring, until it has been absorbed, then ladle in a quarter of the stock. Cook, stirring, until the stock has been absorbed. Gradually add the remaining stock, a little at a time, allowing the rice to absorb the liquid before adding more, and stirring constantly.

4 After about 20 minutes, when all the stock has been absorbed and the rice is cooked but still has a "bite", stir in the butter, saffron water (with the strands) and half the Parmesan. Serve, sprinkled with the remaining Parmesan. Garnish with pink and yellow oyster mushrooms, if you like.

VARIATIONS
There are endless variations on this delectable dish. The proportion of stock to rice, onions, garlic and butter must remain constant but you can ring the changes with the flavourings and cheese.

RISOTTO WITH FOUR VEGETABLES

THIS IS ONE OF THE PRETTIEST RISOTTOS, ESPECIALLY WHEN MADE WITH ACORN SQUASH.

SERVES THREE TO FOUR

INGREDIENTS
115g/4oz/1 cup shelled fresh peas
115g/4oz/1 cup green beans, cut
　into short lengths
30ml/2 tbsp olive oil
75g/3oz/6 tbsp butter
1 acorn squash, skin and seeds
　removed, flesh cut into matchsticks
1 onion, finely chopped
275g/10oz/1½ cups risotto rice
120ml/4fl oz/½ cup Italian dry white
　vermouth
1 litre/1¾ pints/4 cups boiling
　chicken stock
75g/3oz/1 cup freshly grated
　Parmesan cheese
salt and freshly ground black pepper

1 Bring a saucepan of lightly salted water to the boil, add the peas and beans and cook for 2–3 minutes, until the vegetables are just tender. Drain, refresh under cold running water, drain again and set aside.

2 Heat the oil with 25g/1oz/2 tbsp of the butter in a medium saucepan until foaming. Add the squash and cook gently for 2–3 minutes or until just softened. Remove with a slotted spoon and set aside. Add the onion to the pan and cook gently for about 3 minutes, stirring frequently, until softened.

3 Stir in the rice until the grains start to swell and burst, then add the vermouth. Stir until the vermouth stops sizzling and most of it has been absorbed by the rice, then add a few ladlefuls of the stock, with salt and pepper to taste. Stir over a low heat until the stock has been absorbed.

4 Gradually add the remaining stock, a few ladlefuls at a time, allowing the rice to absorb the liquid before adding more, and stirring all the time.

VARIATIONS
Shelled broad beans can be used instead of the peas, and asparagus tips instead of the green beans. Use courgettes if acorn squash is not available.

5 After about 20 minutes, when all the stock has been absorbed and the rice is cooked and creamy but still has a "bite", gently stir in the vegetables, the remaining butter and about half the grated Parmesan. Heat through, then taste for seasoning and serve with the remaining grated Parmesan served separately.

GREEN RISOTTO

YOU COULD USE SPINACH-FLAVOURED RISOTTO RICE TO GIVE THIS STUNNING DISH EVEN GREATER DRAMATIC IMPACT. HOWEVER, WHITE RISOTTO RICE MAKES A PRETTY CONTRAST TO THE SPINACH.

SERVES THREE TO FOUR

INGREDIENTS
    30ml/2 tbsp olive oil
    1 onion, finely chopped
    275g/10oz/1½ cups risotto rice
    1 litre/1¾ pints/4 cups hot chicken
       stock
    75ml/5 tbsp white wine
    about 400g/14oz tender baby
       spinach leaves
    15ml/1 tbsp chopped fresh basil
    5ml/1 tsp chopped fresh mint
    60ml/4 tbsp freshly grated Parmesan
       cheese
    salt and freshly ground black pepper
    knob of butter or more grated
       Parmesan cheese, to serve

1 Heat the oil and fry the onion for 3–4 minutes until soft. Add the rice and stir to coat each grain. Pour in the stock and wine, a little at a time, stirring constantly over a gentle heat until all the liquid has been absorbed.

2 Stir in the spinach leaves and herbs with the last of the liquid, and add a little seasoning. Continue cooking until the rice is tender and the spinach leaves have wilted. Stir in the Parmesan cheese, with a knob of butter, if you like, or serve with extra Parmesan.

COOK'S TIP
The secret with risotto is to add the hot liquid gradually, about a ladleful at a time, and to stir constantly until the liquid has been absorbed before adding more.

RISOTTO WITH BACON, BABY COURGETTES AND PEPPERS

THIS WOULD MAKE THE PERFECT DISH TO COME HOME TO AFTER AN EARLY SHOW AT THE THEATRE. CREAMY RISOTTO TOPPED WITH VEGETABLES AND CRISP BACON IS IRRESISTIBLE AND EASY TO MAKE.

SERVES FOUR

INGREDIENTS
    30ml/2 tbsp olive oil
    115g/4oz rindless streaky bacon
       rashers, cut into thick strips
    350g/12oz/1¾ cups risotto rice
    1.2 litres/2 pints/5 cups hot
       vegetable or chicken stock
    30ml/2 tbsp single cream
    45ml/3 tbsp dry sherry
    50g/2oz/⅔ cup freshly grated
       Parmesan cheese
    50g/2oz/⅔ cup chopped fresh parsley
    salt and freshly ground black pepper
For the vegetables
    1 small red pepper, seeded
    1 small green pepper, seeded
    25g/1oz/2 tbsp butter
    75g/3oz horse mushrooms, sliced
    225g/8oz baby courgettes, halved
    1 onion, halved and sliced
    1 garlic clove, crushed

1 Heat half the oil in a frying pan. Add the bacon and heat gently until the fat runs. Increase the heat and fry until crisp, then drain on kitchen paper and set aside.

2 Heat the remaining oil in a heavy-based saucepan. Add the rice, stir to coat the grains, then ladle in a little of the hot stock. Stir until it has been absorbed. Gradually add the rest of the stock, stirring constantly.

3 Cut the peppers into chunks. Melt the butter in a separate pan and fry the peppers, mushrooms, courgettes, onion and garlic until the onion is just tender. Season well, then stir in the bacon.

4 When all the stock has been absorbed by the rice, stir in the cream, sherry, Parmesan, parsley and seasoning. Spoon the risotto on to individual plates and top each portion with fried vegetables and bacon. Serve immediately.

RISOTTO <u>WITH</u> ASPARAGUS

FRESH FARM ASPARAGUS ONLY HAS A SHORT SEASON, SO IT IS SENSIBLE TO MAKE THE MOST OF IT. THIS ELEGANT RISOTTO IS ABSOLUTELY DELICIOUS.

SERVES THREE TO FOUR

INGREDIENTS
225g/8oz fresh asparagus
750ml/1¼ pints/3 cups vegetable or
  chicken stock
65g/2½oz/5 tbsp butter
1 small onion, finely chopped
275g/10oz/1½ cups risotto rice, such
  as Arborio or Carnaroli
75g/3oz/1 cup freshly grated
  Parmesan cheese
salt and freshly ground black pepper

1 Bring a pan of water to the boil. Cut off any woody pieces on the ends of the asparagus stalks, peel the lower portions, then cook in the water for 5 minutes. Drain the asparagus, reserving the cooking water, refresh under cold water and drain again. Cut the asparagus diagonally into 4cm/1½in pieces. Keep the tip and next-highest sections separate from the stalks.

2 Place the stock in a saucepan and add 450ml/¾ pint/scant 2 cups of the asparagus cooking water. Heat to simmering point, and keep it hot.

3 Melt two-thirds of the butter in a large, heavy-based saucepan or deep frying pan. Add the onion and fry until it is soft and golden. Stir in all the asparagus except the top two sections. Cook for 2–3 minutes. Add the rice and cook for 1–2 minutes, mixing well to coat it with butter. Stir in a ladleful of the hot liquid. Using a wooden spoon, stir until the stock has been absorbed.

4 Gradually add the remaining stock, a little at a time, allowing the rice to absorb the liquid before adding more, and stirring all the time.

5 After 10 minutes, add the remaining asparagus sections. Continue to cook as before, for about 15 minutes, until the rice is *al dente* and the risotto is creamy. Off the heat, stir in the remaining butter and the Parmesan. Grind in a little black pepper, and taste again for salt. Serve at once.

RISOTTO WITH FOUR CHEESES

THIS IS A VERY RICH DISH. SERVE IT FOR A SPECIAL DINNER-PARTY FIRST COURSE, WITH A LIGHT, DRY SPARKLING WHITE WINE.

SERVES FOUR

INGREDIENTS
40g/1½oz/3 tbsp butter
1 small onion, finely chopped
1.2 litres/2 pints/5 cups chicken
  stock, preferably home-made
350g/12oz/1¾ cups risotto rice
200ml/7fl oz/scant 1cup dry white
  wine
50g/2oz/½ cup grated Gruyère cheese
50g/2oz/½ cup diced taleggio cheese
50g/2oz/½ cup diced Gorgonzola
  cheese
50g/2oz/⅔ cup freshly grated
  Parmesan cheese
salt and freshly ground black pepper
chopped fresh flat leaf parsley, to
  garnish

1 Melt the butter in a large, heavy-based saucepan or deep frying pan and fry the onion over a gentle heat for about 4–5 minutes, stirring frequently, until softened and lightly browned. Pour the stock into another pan and heat it to simmering point.

2 Add the rice to the onion mixture, stir until the grains start to swell and burst, then add the wine. Stir until it stops sizzling and most of it has been absorbed by the rice, then pour in a little of the hot stock. Add salt and pepper to taste. Stir over a low heat until the stock has been absorbed.

3 Gradually add the remaining stock, a little at a time, allowing the rice to absorb the liquid before adding more, and stirring constantly. After 20–25 minutes the rice will be *al dente* and the risotto creamy.

4 Turn off the heat under the pan, then add the Gruyère, taleggio, Gorgonzola and 30ml/2 tbsp of the Parmesan cheese. Stir gently until the cheeses have melted, then taste for seasoning. Spoon into a serving bowl and garnish with parsley. Serve the remaining Parmesan separately.

TIMBALLO OF RICE WITH PEAS

THE TIMBALLO GETS ITS NAME FROM THE FACT THAT IT LOOKS LIKE AN INVERTED KETTLEDRUM (TIMBALLO OR TIMPANO). IT IS MADE LIKE A RISOTTO, BUT IS GIVEN A FINAL BAKING IN THE OVEN.

SERVES THREE TO FOUR

INGREDIENTS
  75g/3oz/6 tbsp butter
  30ml/2 tbsp olive oil
  1 small onion, finely chopped
  50g/2oz ham, cut into small dice
  45ml/3 tbsp finely chopped fresh
    parsley, plus a few sprigs to garnish
  2 garlic cloves, very finely chopped
  225g/8oz/2 cups shelled peas,
    thawed if frozen
  60ml/4 tbsp water
  1.3 litres/2¼ pints/5½ cups chicken
    or vegetable stock
  350g/12oz/1¾ cups risotto rice,
    preferably Arborio
  75g/3oz/1 cup freshly grated
    Parmesan cheese
  175g/6oz fontina cheese, very
    thinly sliced

1 Preheat the oven to 180°C/350°F/ Gas 4. Heat half the butter and all the oil in a large, heavy-based pan. Cook the onion until soft, then add the ham and stir over a medium heat for 3–4 minutes. Stir in the parsley and garlic. Cook for 2 minutes. Add the peas, then season and add the water.

2 Cover the pan, and cook for 8 minutes for fresh peas, or 4 minutes for frozen peas. Remove the lid and cook until the liquid has evaporated. Spoon half the mixture into a dish. Heat the stock and keep it simmering. Butter a flat-based baking dish and line with non-stick baking paper.

3 Stir the rice into the pea mixture in the pan. Heat through, then add a ladleful of stock. Cook until this has been absorbed, stirring constantly. Add the remaining stock in the same way, adding more liquid only when the previous quantity has been absorbed.

4 After about 20 minutes, when the rice is just tender, remove it from the heat. Season and mix in most of the remaining butter and half the Parmesan.

5 Assemble the timballo. Sprinkle the bottom of the dish with Parmesan, and spoon in half the rice. Add a layer of fontina slices and spoon over the reserved pea and ham mixture. Smooth level, and sprinkle with Parmesan.

6 Cover with the remaining fontina slices and end with the remaining rice. Sprinkle with the last of the Parmesan, and dot with butter. Bake for 10–15 minutes. Remove from the oven, and allow to stand for 10 minutes.

7 To unmould, slip a knife around the timballo between the rice and the dish. Place a serving plate upside down on top. Wearing oven gloves, turn over dish and plate together. Peel off the lining paper. Serve by cutting into wedges.

LEMON AND HERB RISOTTO CAKE

THIS UNUSUAL DISH CAN BE SERVED AS A MAIN COURSE WITH SALAD, OR AS A SATISFYING SIDE DISH. IT IS ALSO GOOD SERVED COLD, AND PACKS WELL FOR PICNICS.

SERVES FOUR

INGREDIENTS
  1 small leek, finely sliced
  600ml/1 pint/2½ cups chicken stock
  225g/8oz/generous 1 cup risotto rice
  finely grated rind of 1 lemon
  30ml/2 tbsp snipped fresh chives
  30ml/2 tbsp chopped fresh parsley
  75g/3oz/¾ cup grated mozzarella
    cheese
  salt and freshly ground black pepper

1 Preheat the oven to 200°C/400°F/ Gas 6. Lightly oil a 21cm/8½in round loose-based cake tin.

2 Put the leek in a large pan with 45ml/3 tbsp of the stock. Cook over a medium heat, stirring occasionally, until softened. Stir in the rice, then add the remaining stock.

3 Bring to the boil. Lower the heat, cover the pan and simmer gently, stirring occasionally, for about 20 minutes, or until all the liquid has been absorbed.

4 Stir in the lemon rind, herbs, cheese, and seasoning. Spoon the mixture into the tin, cover with foil and bake for 30–35 minutes or until lightly browned. Leave to stand for 5 minutes, then turn out. Serve hot or cold, in slices.

COOK'S TIP
This risotto uses less liquid than normal and therefore has a drier consistency.

RISOTTO WITH PRAWNS

THIS PRAWN RISOTTO IS GIVEN A SOFT PINK COLOUR BY THE ADDITION OF A LITTLE TOMATO PURÉE.

<u>SERVES THREE TO FOUR</u>

INGREDIENTS
  350g/12oz large raw prawns, in
    the shells
  1 litres/1¾ pints/4 cups water
  1 bay leaf
  1–2 fresh parsley sprigs
  5ml/1 tsp whole peppercorns
  2 garlic cloves, peeled and left whole
  65g/2½oz/5 tbsp butter
  2 shallots, finely chopped
  275g/10oz/1½ cups risotto rice
  15ml/1 tbsp tomato purée softened
    in 120ml/4fl oz/½ cup dry white
    wine
  salt and freshly ground black pepper

1 Put the prawns in a large saucepan and add the water, herbs, peppercorns and garlic. Bring to the boil over a medium heat. As soon as the prawns turn pink, lift them out, peel them and return the shells to the saucepan. Boil the stock with the shells for 10 minutes more, then strain. Return the stock to the clean pan, and simmer gently until needed.

2 Slice the prawns in half lengthways, removing the dark vein along the back. Set four halves aside for the garnish, and roughly chop the rest.

3 Heat two-thirds of the butter in a flameproof casserole and fry the shallots until golden. Add the rice, mixing well to coat it with butter. Pour in the tomato purée and wine and cook until it has been absorbed. Add the simmering stock, a ladleful at a time, allowing it to be absorbed before adding more.

4 When all the stock has been absorbed and the rice is creamy, stir in the chopped prawns, the remaining butter and seasoning. Cover and let the risotto rest for 3–4 minutes. Spoon into a bowl, garnish with the reserved prawns and serve.

MUSHROOM RISOTTO

MUSHROOM RISOTTO IS EASY TO MAKE AND APPEALS TO ALMOST EVERYONE. WILD MUSHROOMS WILL GIVE A MORE INTENSE FLAVOUR, BUT YOU CAN USE WHATEVER MUSHROOMS ARE AVAILABLE.

<u>SERVES THREE TO FOUR</u>

INGREDIENTS
  25g/1oz/⅓ cup dried wild
    mushrooms, preferably porcini
  350ml/12fl oz/1½ cups warm water
  900ml/1½ pints/3¾ cups beef or
    chicken stock
  175g/6oz/1½–2 cups button
    mushrooms, sliced
  juice of ½ lemon
  75g/3oz/6 tbsp butter
  30ml/2 tbsp finely chopped fresh
    parsley
  30ml/2 tbsp olive oil
  1 small onion, finely chopped
  275g/10oz/1½ cups risotto rice
  120ml/4fl oz/½ cup dry white wine
  45ml/3 tbsp freshly grated Parmesan
    cheese
  salt and freshly ground black pepper
  fresh herbs, to garnish

1 Put the dried mushrooms in a bowl with the warm water. Soak them for at least 40 minutes, then lift them out and rinse them thoroughly. Filter the soaking water through a strainer lined with kitchen paper, and pour into a saucepan. Add the stock to the pan and bring to simmering point.

2 Toss the button mushrooms with the lemon juice in a bowl. Melt a third of the butter in a saucepan and fry the button mushrooms until they give up their juices and begin to brown. Stir in the parsley, cook for 30 seconds more, then transfer to a bowl.

3 Heat the olive oil and half the remaining butter in the saucepan and fry the onion until soft. Add the rice and stir constantly, so that the grains are evenly coated in the oil.

4 Stir in all of the mushrooms, add the wine, and cook over a medium heat until it has been absorbed. Add the stock, a ladleful at a time, making sure each is absorbed before adding more. When all the liquid has been absorbed, remove the pan from the heat, stir in the remaining butter, the Parmesan and seasoning. Cover the pan and allow to rest for 3–4 minutes before serving.

RISOTTO ALLA MILANESE

THIS CLASSIC RISOTTO IS ALWAYS SERVED WITH THE HEARTY BEEF STEW, OSSO BUCO, BUT ALSO MAKES A DELICIOUS FIRST COURSE OR LIGHT SUPPER DISH IN ITS OWN RIGHT.

SERVES THREE TO FOUR

INGREDIENTS

    about 1.2 litres/2 pints/5 cups beef
      or chicken stock
    good pinch of saffron strands
    75g/3oz/6 tbsp butter
    1 onion, finely chopped
    275g/10oz/1½ cups risotto rice
    75g/3oz/1 cup freshly grated
      Parmesan cheese
    salt and freshly ground black pepper

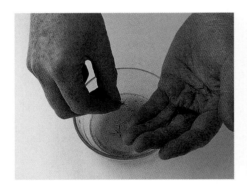

1 Bring the stock to the boil, then reduce to a low simmer. Ladle a little stock into a small bowl. Add the saffron strands and leave to infuse.

2 Melt 50g/2oz/4 tbsp of the butter in a large saucepan until foaming. Add the onion and cook gently for about 3 minutes, stirring frequently, until softened but not browned.

3 Add the rice. Stir until the grains start to swell and burst, then add a few ladlefuls of the stock, with the saffron liquid and salt and pepper to taste. Stir over a low heat until the stock has been absorbed. Add the remaining stock, a few ladlefuls at a time, allowing the rice to absorb all the liquid before adding more, and stirring constantly. After 20–25 minutes, the rice should be just tender and the risotto golden yellow, moist and creamy.

4 Gently stir in about two-thirds of the grated Parmesan and the remaining butter. Heat through until the butter has melted, then taste for seasoning. Transfer the risotto to a warmed serving bowl or platter and serve hot, with the remaining grated Parmesan served separately.

RISI E BISI

A CLASSIC PEA AND HAM RISOTTO FROM THE VENETO. ALTHOUGH THIS IS TRADITIONALLY SERVED AS A STARTER IN ITALY, IT ALSO MAKES AN EXCELLENT SUPPER DISH WITH HOT, CRUSTY BREAD.

SERVES FOUR

INGREDIENTS

75g/3oz/6 tbsp butter
1 small onion, finely chopped
about 1 litre/1¾ pints/4 cups
  simmering chicken stock
275g/10oz/1½ cups risotto rice
150ml/¼ pint/⅔ cup dry white wine
225g/8oz/2 cups frozen petits pois,
  thawed
115g/4oz cooked ham, diced
salt and freshly ground black pepper
50g/2oz/⅔ cup freshly grated
  Parmesan cheese, to serve

1 Melt 50g/2oz/4 tbsp of the butter in a saucepan until foaming. Add the onion and cook gently for about 3 minutes, stirring frequently, until softened. Have the hot stock ready in an adjacent pan.

2 Add the rice to the onion mixture. Stir until the grains start to swell, then pour in the wine. Stir until it stops sizzling and most of it has been absorbed, then pour in a little hot stock, with salt and pepper to taste. Stir continuously, over a low heat, until all the stock has been absorbed.

3 Add the remaining stock, a little at a time, allowing the rice to absorb all the liquid before adding more, and stirring constantly. Add the peas after about 20 minutes. After 25–30 minutes, the rice should be *al dente* and the risotto moist and creamy.

4 Gently stir in the diced cooked ham and the remaining butter. Heat through until the butter has melted, then taste for seasoning. Transfer to a warmed serving bowl. Grate or shave a little Parmesan over the top and serve the rest separately.

COOK'S TIP
Always use fresh Parmesan cheese, grated off a block. It has a far superior flavour to the ready-grated Parmesan.

RISOTTO WITH CHICKEN

THIS IS A CLASSIC COMBINATION OF CHICKEN AND RICE, COOKED WITH PARMA HAM, WHITE WINE AND PARMESAN CHEESE.

SERVES SIX

INGREDIENTS
  30ml/2 tbsp olive oil
  225g/8oz skinless, boneless chicken
    breasts, cut into 2.5cm/1in cubes
  1 onion, finely chopped
  1 garlic clove, finely chopped
  450g/1lb/2⅓ cups risotto rice
  120ml/4fl oz/½ cup dry white wine
  1.5ml/¼ tsp saffron threads
  1.75 litres/3 pints/7½ cups
    simmering chicken stock
  50g/2oz Parma ham, cut into thin
    strips
  25g/1oz/2 tbsp butter, cubed
  25g/1oz/⅓ cup freshly grated
    Parmesan cheese, plus extra to
    serve
salt and freshly ground black pepper
flat leaf parsley, to garnish

1 Heat the oil in a frying pan over a moderately high heat. Add the chicken cubes and cook, stirring, until they start to turn white.

2 Reduce the heat to low and add the onion and garlic. Cook, stirring, until the onion is soft. Stir in the rice. Sauté for 1–2 minutes, stirring constantly, until all the rice grains are coated in oil.

3 Add the wine and cook, stirring, until the wine has been absorbed. Stir the saffron into the simmering stock, then add ladlefuls of stock to the rice, allowing each ladleful to be absorbed before adding the next.

4 When the rice is three-quarters cooked, add the Parma ham and continue cooking until the rice is just tender and the risotto creamy.

5 Add the butter and the Parmesan and stir in well. Season with salt and pepper to taste. Serve the risotto hot, sprinkled with a little more Parmesan, and garnish with parsley.

RISOTTO WITH SMOKED BACON AND TOMATO

A CLASSIC RISOTTO, WITH PLENTY OF ONIONS, SMOKED BACON AND SUN-DRIED TOMATOES. YOU'LL WANT TO KEEP GOING BACK FOR MORE!

SERVES FOUR TO SIX

INGREDIENTS

8 sun-dried tomatoes in olive oil
275g/10oz good-quality rindless
  smoked back bacon
75g/3oz/6 tbsp butter
450g/1lb onions, roughly chopped
2 garlic cloves, crushed
350g/12oz/1¾ cups risotto rice
300ml/½ pint/1¼ cups dry white wine
1 litre/1¾ pints/4 cups simmering
  vegetable stock
50g/2oz/⅔ cup freshly grated
  Parmesan cheese
45ml/3 tbsp mixed chopped fresh
  chives and flat leaf parsley
salt and freshly ground black pepper

1 Drain the sun-dried tomatoes and reserve 15ml/1 tbsp of the oil. Roughly chop the tomatoes and set aside. Cut the bacon into 2.5cm/1in pieces.

2 Heat the oil from the sun-dried tomatoes in a large saucepan. Fry the bacon until well cooked and golden. Remove with a slotted spoon and drain on kitchen paper.

3 Heat 25g/1oz/2 tbsp of the butter in a saucepan and fry the onions and garlic over a medium heat for 10 minutes, until soft and golden brown.

4 Stir in the rice. Cook for 1 minute, until the grains turn translucent. Stir the wine into the stock. Add a ladleful of the mixture to the rice and cook gently until the liquid has been absorbed.

5 Stir in another ladleful of the stock and wine mixture and allow it to be absorbed. Repeat this process until all the liquid has been used up. This should take 25–30 minutes. The risotto will turn thick and creamy, and the rice should be tender but not sticky.

6 Just before serving, stir in the bacon, sun-dried tomatoes, Parmesan, half the herbs and the remaining butter. Adjust the seasoning (remember that the bacon may be quite salty) and serve sprinkled with the remaining herbs.

SHELLFISH RISOTTO <u>WITH</u> MIXED MUSHROOMS

THIS IS A QUICK AND EASY RISOTTO, WHERE ALL THE LIQUID IS ADDED IN ONE GO. THE METHOD IS WELL-SUITED TO THIS SHELLFISH DISH, AS IT MEANS EVERYTHING COOKS TOGETHER UNDISTURBED.

SERVES SIX

INGREDIENTS

225g/8oz live mussels
225g/8oz live Venus or carpet shell clams
45ml/3 tbsp olive oil
1 onion, chopped
450g/1lb/2⅓ cups risotto rice
1.75 litres/3 pints/7½ cups simmering chicken or vegetable stock
150ml/¼ pint/⅔ cup white wine
225g/8oz/2–3 cups assorted wild and cultivated mushrooms, trimmed and sliced
115g/4oz raw peeled prawns, deveined
1 medium or 2 small squid, cleaned, trimmed and sliced
3 drops truffle oil (optional)
75ml/5 tbsp chopped mixed fresh parsley and chervil
celery salt and cayenne pepper

1 Scrub the mussels and clams clean and discard any that are open and do not close when tapped with a knife. Set aside. Heat the oil in a large frying pan and fry the onion for 6–8 minutes until soft but not browned.

2 Add the rice, stirring to coat the grains in oil, then pour in the stock and wine and cook for 5 minutes. Add the mushrooms and cook for 5 minutes more, stirring occasionally.

3 Add the prawns, squid, mussels and clams and stir into the rice. Cover the pan and simmer over a low heat for 15 minutes until the prawns have turned pink and the mussels and clams have opened. Discard any of the shellfish that remain closed.

4 Switch off the heat. Add the truffle oil, if using, and stir in the herbs. Cover tightly and leave to stand for 5–10 minutes to allow all the flavours to blend. Season to taste with celery salt and a pinch of cayenne, pile into a warmed dish, and serve immediately.

SALMON RISOTTO <u>WITH</u> CUCUMBER <u>AND</u> TARRAGON

THIS SIMPLE RISOTTO IS COOKED ALL IN ONE GO, AND IS THEREFORE SIMPLER THAN THE USUAL RISOTTO. IF YOU PREFER TO COOK THE TRADITIONAL WAY, ADD THE LIQUID GRADUALLY, ADDING THE SALMON ABOUT TWO-THIRDS OF THE WAY THROUGH COOKING.

SERVES FOUR

INGREDIENTS

25g/1oz/2 tbsp butter
small bunch of spring onions, white parts only, chopped
½ cucumber, peeled, seeded and chopped
350g/12oz/1¾ cups risotto rice
1.2 litres/2 pints/5 cups hot chicken or fish stock
150ml/¼ pint/⅔ cup dry white wine
450g/1lb salmon fillet, skinned and diced
45ml/3 tbsp chopped fresh tarragon
salt and freshly ground black pepper

1 Heat the butter in a large saucepan and add the spring onions and cucumber. Cook for 2–3 minutes without letting the spring onions colour.

2 Stir in the rice, then pour in the stock and wine. Bring to the boil, then lower the heat and simmer, uncovered, for 10 minutes, stirring occasionally.

3 Stir in the diced salmon and season to taste with salt and freshly ground black pepper. Continue cooking for a further 5 minutes, stirring occasionally, then switch off the heat. Cover and leave to stand for 5 minutes.

4 Remove the lid, add the chopped tarragon and mix lightly. Spoon into a warmed bowl and serve.

VARIATION
Carnaroli risotto rice would be excellent in this risotto, although if it is not available, Arborio can be used instead.

Truffle and Lobster Risotto

To capture the precious qualities of the fresh truffle, partner it with lobster and serve in a silky smooth risotto. Both truffle shavings and truffle oil are added towards the end of cooking to preserve their flavour.

SERVES FOUR

INGREDIENTS
  50g/2oz/4 tbsp unsalted butter
  1 medium onion, chopped
  350g/12oz/1¾ cups risotto rice,
    preferably Carnaroli
  1 fresh thyme sprig
  150ml/¼ pint/⅔ cup dry white wine
  1.2 litres/2 pints/5 cups simmering
    chicken stock
  1 freshly cooked lobster
  45ml/3 tbsp chopped mixed fresh
    parsley and chervil
  3–4 drops truffle oil
  2 hard-boiled eggs
  1 fresh black or white truffle
  salt and freshly ground black pepper

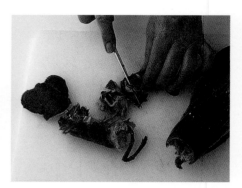

1 Melt the butter, add the onion and fry until soft. Add the rice and stir well to coat with fat. Add the thyme, then the wine, and cook until it has been absorbed. Add the chicken stock a little at a time, stirring. Let each ladleful be absorbed before adding the next.

2 Twist off the lobster tail, cut the underside with scissors and remove the white tail meat. Carefully break open the claws with a small kitchen hammer and remove the flesh. Cut half the meat into big chunks, then roughly chop the remainder.

3 Stir in the chopped lobster meat, half the chopped herbs and the truffle oil. Remove the rice from the heat, cover and leave to stand for 5 minutes.

4 Divide among warmed plates and centre the lobster chunks on top. Cut the hard-boiled eggs into wedges and arrange them around the lobster meat. Finally, shave fresh truffle over each portion and sprinkle with the remaining herbs. Serve immediately.

COOK'S TIP
To make the most of the aromatic truffle scent, keep the tuber in the rice jar for a few days before use.

PANCETTA AND BROAD BEAN RISOTTO

THIS DELICIOUS RISOTTO MAKES A HEALTHY AND FILLING MEAL, SERVED WITH COOKED FRESH SEASONAL VEGETABLES OR A MIXED GREEN SALAD.

SERVES FOUR

INGREDIENTS
 15ml/1 tbsp olive oil
 1 onion, chopped
 2 garlic cloves, finely chopped
 175g/6oz smoked pancetta, diced
 350g/12oz/1¾ cups risotto rice
 1.5 litres/2½ pints/6¼ cups
  simmering chicken stock
 225g/8oz/2 cups frozen baby broad
  beans
 30ml/2 tbsp chopped fresh mixed
  herbs, such as parsley, thyme and
  oregano
 salt and freshly ground black pepper
 shavings of Parmesan cheese, to
  serve

1 Heat the oil in a large saucepan. Add the onion, garlic and pancetta and cook gently for about 5 minutes, stirring occasionally. Do not allow the onion and garlic to brown.

2 Add the rice to the pan and cook for 1 minute, stirring. Add a ladleful of stock and cook, stirring all the time, until the liquid has been absorbed.

3 Continue adding the stock, a ladleful at a time, until the rice is tender, and almost all the liquid has been absorbed. This will take 30–35 minutes.

4 Meanwhile, cook the broad beans in a saucepan of lightly salted, boiling water for about 3 minutes until tender. Drain well and stir into the risotto, with the mixed herbs. Add salt and pepper to taste. Spoon into a bowl and serve, sprinkled with shavings of fresh Parmesan cheese.

COOK'S TIP
If the broad beans are large, or if you prefer skinned beans, remove the outer skin after cooking.

BROWN RICE RISOTTO WITH MUSHROOMS AND PARMESAN

A CLASSIC RISOTTO OF MIXED MUSHROOMS, HERBS AND FRESH PARMESAN CHEESE, BUT MADE USING BROWN LONG GRAIN RICE. SERVE SIMPLY, WITH A MIXED LEAF SALAD TOSSED IN A LIGHT DRESSING.

SERVES FOUR

INGREDIENTS

15ml/1 tbsp olive oil
4 shallots, finely chopped
2 garlic cloves, crushed
15g/½oz/2 tbsp dried porcini
   mushrooms, soaked in 150ml/
   ¼ pint/⅔ cup hot water for 20
   minutes
250g/9oz/1⅓ cups brown long grain
   rice
900ml/1½ pints/3¾ cups
   well-flavoured vegetable stock
450g/1lb/6 cups mixed mushrooms,
   such as closed cup, chestnut and
   field mushrooms, sliced if large
30–45ml/2–3 tbsp chopped fresh flat
   leaf parsley
50g/2oz/⅔ cup freshly grated
   Parmesan cheese
salt and freshly ground black pepper

1 Heat the oil in a large saucepan, add the shallots and garlic and cook gently for 5 minutes, stirring. Drain the porcini, reserving their liquid, and chop roughly. Add the brown rice to the shallot mixture and stir to coat the grains in oil.

2 Stir the vegetable stock and the porcini soaking liquid into the rice mixture in the saucepan. Bring to the boil, lower the heat and simmer, uncovered, for about 20 minutes or until most of the liquid has been absorbed, stirring frequently.

3 Add all the mushrooms, stir well, and cook the risotto for 10–15 minutes more until the liquid has been absorbed.

4 Season with salt and pepper to taste, stir in the chopped parsley and grated Parmesan and serve at once.

CRAB RISOTTO

THIS IS A FRESH-FLAVOURED RISOTTO WHICH MAKES A WONDERFUL MAIN COURSE OR STARTER.
YOU WILL NEED TWO CRABS FOR THIS RECIPE, AND IT IS THEREFORE A GOOD DISH TO FOLLOW
A VISIT TO THE SEASIDE, WHERE CRABS ARE CHEAP AND PLENTIFUL.

SERVES THREE TO FOUR

INGREDIENTS

2 large cooked crabs
15ml/1 tbsp olive oil
25g/1oz/2 tbsp butter
2 shallots, finely chopped
275g/10oz/1½ cups risotto rice,
  preferably Carnaroli
75ml/5 tbsp Marsala or brandy
1 litre/1¾ pints/4 cups simmering
  fish stock
5ml/1 tsp chopped fresh tarragon
5ml/1 tsp chopped fresh parsley
60ml/4 tbsp double cream
salt and freshly ground black pepper

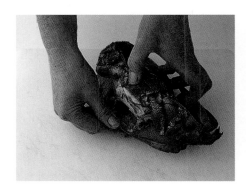

1 First remove the crab meat from each of the shells in turn. Hold the crab firmly in one hand and hit the back underside firmly with the heel of your hand. This should loosen the shell from the body. Using your thumbs, push against the body and pull away from the shell. From the inside of the shell, remove and discard the intestines.

2 Discard the grey gills (dead man's fingers). Break off the claws and legs from the body, then use a small hammer or crackers to break them open. Using a pick, remove the meat from the claws and legs. Place the meat on a plate.

3 Using a pick or a skewer, pick out the white meat from the body cavities and place on the plate with the meat from the claws and legs, reserving some white meat to garnish. Scoop out the brown meat from inside the shell and set aside with the white meat on the plate.

4 Heat the oil and butter in a pan and gently fry the shallots until soft but not browned. Add the rice. Cook for a few minutes, stirring, until the rice is slightly translucent, then add the Marsala or brandy, bring to the boil, and cook, stirring, until the liquid has evaporated.

5 Add a ladleful of hot stock and cook, stirring, until all the stock has been absorbed. Continue cooking in this way until about two-thirds of the stock has been added, then carefully stir in all the crab meat and the herbs.

6 Continue to cook the risotto, adding the remaining stock. When the rice is almost cooked but still has a slight "bite", remove it from the heat, stir in the cream and adjust the seasoning. Cover and leave to stand for 3 minutes to finish cooking. Serve garnished with the reserved white crab meat.

MONKFISH RISOTTO

MONKFISH IS A VERSATILE, FIRM-TEXTURED FISH WITH A SUPERB FLAVOUR, WHICH IS ACCENTUATED WITH LEMON GRASS IN THIS SOPHISTICATED RISOTTO.

SERVES THREE TO FOUR

INGREDIENTS
seasoned flour
about 450g/1lb monkfish, cut into
    cubes
30ml/2 tbsp olive oil
40g/1½oz/3 tbsp butter
2 shallots, finely chopped
1 lemon grass stalk, finely chopped
275g/10oz/1½ cups risotto rice,
    preferably Carnaroli
175ml/6fl oz/¾ cup dry white wine
1 litre/1¾ pints/4 cups simmering
    fish stock
30ml/2 tbsp chopped fresh parsley
salt and white pepper
dressed salad leaves, to serve

4 Tip in the rice. Cook for 2–3 minutes, stirring, until the rice is coated with oil and is slightly translucent. Gradually add the wine and the hot stock, stirring and waiting until each ladleful has been absorbed before adding the next.

5 When the rice is about three-quarters cooked, stir in the monkfish. Continue to cook the risotto, adding the remaining stock and stirring constantly until the grains of rice are tender, but still retain a bit of "bite". Season with salt and white pepper.

6 Remove the pan from the heat, stir in the parsley and cover with the lid. Leave the risotto to stand for a few minutes before serving with a garnish of dressed salad leaves.

COOK'S TIP
Lemon grass adds a subtle flavour to this dish. Remove the tough outer skin and chop the inner flesh finely.

1 Spoon the seasoned flour over the monkfish cubes in a bowl. Toss the monkfish until coated.

2 Heat 15ml/1 tbsp of the oil with half the butter in a frying pan. Fry the monkfish cubes over a medium to high heat for 3–4 minutes until cooked, turning occasionally. Transfer to a plate and set aside.

3 Heat the remaining oil and butter in a saucepan and fry the shallots over a low heat for about 4 minutes until soft but not brown. Add the lemon grass and cook for 1–2 minutes more.

SCALLOP RISOTTO

TRY TO BUY FRESH SCALLOPS FOR THIS DISH, WHICH TASTE MUCH BETTER THAN FROZEN ONES.
FRESH SCALLOPS COME WITH THE CORAL ATTACHED, WHICH ADDS FLAVOUR, TEXTURE AND COLOUR.

SERVES THREE TO FOUR

INGREDIENTS
    about 12 scallops, with their corals
    50g/2oz/4 tbsp butter
    15ml/1 tbsp olive oil
    30ml/2 tbsp Pernod
    2 shallots, finely chopped
    275g/10oz/1½ cups risotto rice
    1 litre/1¾ pints/4 cups simmering
      fish stock
    generous pinch of saffron strands,
      dissolved in 15ml/1 tbsp warm milk
    30ml/2 tbsp chopped fresh parsley
    60ml/4 tbsp double cream
    salt and freshly ground black pepper

1 Separate the scallops from their corals. Cut the white flesh in half or into 2cm/¾in slices.

2 Melt half the butter with 5ml/1 tsp oil. Fry the white parts of the scallops for 2–3 minutes. Pour over the Pernod, heat for a few seconds, then ignite and allow to flame for a few seconds. When the flames have died down, remove the pan from the heat.

3 Heat the remaining butter and olive oil in a pan and fry the shallots for about 3–4 minutes, until soft but not browned. Add the rice and cook for a few minutes, stirring, until the rice is coated with oil and is beginning to turn translucent around the edges.

4 Gradually add the hot stock, a ladleful at a time, stirring constantly and waiting for each ladleful of stock to be absorbed before adding the next.

5 When the rice is very nearly cooked, add the scallops and all the juices from the pan, together with the corals, the saffron milk, parsley and seasoning. Stir well to mix. Continue cooking, adding the remaining stock and stirring occasionally, until the risotto is thick and creamy.

6 Remove the pan from the heat, stir in the double cream and cover. Leave the risotto to rest for about 3 minutes to complete the cooking, then pile it into a warmed bowl and serve.

SQUID RISOTTO WITH CHILLI AND CORIANDER

Squid needs to be cooked either very quickly or very slowly. Here the squid is marinated in lime and kiwi fruit — a popular method in New Zealand for tenderising squid.

SERVES THREE TO FOUR

INGREDIENTS
   about 450g/1lb squid
   about 45ml/3 tbsp olive oil
   15g/½oz/1 tbsp butter
   1 onion, finely chopped
   2 garlic cloves, crushed
   1 fresh red chilli, seeded and finely
      sliced
   275g/10oz/1½ cups risotto rice
   175ml/6fl oz/¾ cup dry white wine
   1 litre/1¾ pints/4 cups simmering
      fish stock
   30ml/2 tbsp chopped fresh coriander
   salt and freshly ground black pepper
For the marinade
   2 ripe kiwi fruit, chopped and mashed
   1 fresh red chilli, seeded and finely
      sliced
   30ml/2 tbsp fresh lime juice

1 If not already cleaned, prepare the squid by cutting off the tentacles at the base and pulling to remove the quill. Discard the quill and intestines, if necessary, and pull away the thin outer skin. Rinse the body and cut into thin strips: cut the tentacles into short pieces, discarding the beak and eyes.

2 Mash the kiwi fruit for the marinade in a bowl, then stir in the chilli and lime juice. Add the squid, stirring to coat all the strips in the mixture. Season with salt and freshly ground black pepper, cover with clear film and set aside in the fridge for 4 hours or overnight.

3 Drain the squid. Heat 15ml/1 tbsp of the olive oil in a frying pan and cook the strips, in batches if necessary, for about 30–60 seconds over a high heat. It is important that the squid cooks very quickly. Transfer the cooked squid to a plate and set aside. Don't worry if some of the marinade clings to the squid, but if too much juice accumulates in the pan, pour this into a jug and add more olive oil when cooking the next batch, so that the squid fries rather than simmers. Reserve the accumulated juices in a jug.

4 Heat the remaining oil with the butter in a large saucepan and gently fry the onion and garlic for 5–6 minutes until soft. Add the sliced chilli to the saucepan and fry for 1 minute more.

5 Add the rice. Cook for a few minutes, stirring, until the rice is coated with oil and is slightly translucent, then stir in the wine until it has been absorbed.

6 Gradually add the hot stock and the reserved cooking liquid from the squid, a ladleful at a time, stirring the rice constantly and waiting until each quantity of stock has been absorbed before adding the next.

7 When the rice is about three-quarters cooked, stir in the squid and continue cooking the risotto until all the stock has been absorbed and the rice is tender, but retains a bit of "bite". Stir in the chopped coriander, cover with the lid or a dish towel, and leave to rest for a few minutes before serving.

COOK'S TIP
Although fish stock underlines the flavour of the squid, a light chicken or vegetable stock would also work well in this recipe.

MUSSEL RISOTTO

FRESH ROOT GINGER AND CORIANDER ADD A DISTINCTIVE FLAVOUR TO THIS DISH, WHILE THE GREEN CHILLIES GIVE IT A LITTLE HEAT. THE CHILLIES COULD BE OMITTED FOR A MILDER DISH.

SERVES THREE TO FOUR

INGREDIENTS
- 900g/2lb fresh mussels
- about 250ml/8fl oz/1 cup dry white wine
- 30ml/2 tbsp olive oil
- 1 onion, chopped
- 2 garlic cloves, crushed
- 1–2 fresh green chillies, seeded and finely sliced
- 2.5cm/1in piece of fresh root ginger, grated
- 275g/10oz/1½ cups risotto rice
- 900ml/1½ pints/3¾ cups simmering fish stock
- 30ml/2 tbsp chopped fresh coriander
- 30ml/2 tbsp double cream
- salt and freshly ground black pepper

1 Scrub the mussels, discarding any that do not close when sharply tapped. Place in a large saucepan. Add 120ml/4fl oz/½ cup of the wine and bring to the boil. Cover the pan and cook the mussels for 4–5 minutes until they have opened, shaking the pan occasionally. Drain, reserving the liquid and discarding any mussels that have not opened. Remove most of the mussels from their shells, reserving a few in their shells for decoration. Strain the mussel liquid.

2 Heat the oil and fry the onion and garlic for 3–4 minutes until beginning to soften. Add the chillies. Continue to cook over a low heat for 1–2 minutes, stirring frequently, then stir in the ginger and fry gently for 1 minute more.

3 Add the rice and cook over a medium heat for 2 minutes, stirring, until the rice is coated in oil and becomes translucent.

4 Stir in the reserved cooking liquid from the mussels. When this has been absorbed, add the remaining wine and cook stirring, until this has been absorbed. Now add the hot fish stock, a little at a time, making sure each addition has been absorbed before adding the next.

5 When the rice is about three-quarters cooked, stir in the mussels. Add the coriander and season with salt and pepper. Continue adding stock to the risotto until it is creamy and the rice is tender but slightly firm in the centre.

6 Remove the risotto from the heat, stir in the cream, cover and leave to rest for a few minutes. Spoon into a warmed serving dish, decorate with the reserved mussels in their shells, and serve immediately.

SEAFOOD RISOTTO

*YOU CAN USE ANY SHELLFISH OR SEAFOOD FOR THIS RISOTTO, AS LONG AS THE TOTAL WEIGHT IS
SIMILAR TO THAT USED HERE. THE RISOTTO WOULD ALSO MAKE A VERY GOOD STARTER FOR EIGHT.*

SERVES FOUR TO SIX

INGREDIENTS

450g/1lb fresh mussels
about 250ml/8fl oz/1 cup dry white
  wine
225g/8oz sea bass fillet, skinned and
  cut into pieces
seasoned flour
60ml/4 tbsp olive oil
8 scallops with corals separated,
  white parts halved or sliced, if large
225g/8oz squid, cleaned and cut
  into rings
12 large raw prawns or langoustines,
  heads removed
2 shallots, finely chopped
1 garlic clove, crushed
400g/14oz/2 cups risotto rice,
  preferably Carnaroli
3 tomatoes, peeled, seeded and
  chopped
1.5 litres/2½ pints/6¼ cups
  simmering fish stock
30ml/2 tbsp chopped fresh parsley
30ml/2 tbsp double cream
salt and freshly ground black pepper

1 Scrub the mussels, discarding any that do not close when sharply tapped. Place them in a large saucepan and add 90ml/6 tbsp of the wine. Bring to the boil, cover the pan and cook for 3–4 minutes until all the mussels have opened, shaking the pan occasionally. Drain, reserving the liquid and discarding any mussels that have not opened. Set aside a few mussels in their shells for garnishing; remove the others from their shells. Strain the cooking liquid.

2 Dust the pieces of sea bass in seasoned flour. Heat 30ml/2 tbsp of the olive oil in a frying pan and fry the fish for 3–4 minutes until cooked. Transfer to a plate. Add a little more oil to the pan and fry the white parts of the scallops for 1–2 minutes on both sides until tender. Transfer to a plate.

3 Fry the squid for 3–4 minutes in the same pan, adding a little more oil if necessary, then set aside. Lastly, add the prawns or langoustines and fry for a further 3–4 minutes until pink, turning frequently. Towards the end of cooking, add a splash of wine – about 30ml/ 2 tbsp – and continue cooking so that the prawns become tender, but do not burn. Remove the prawns from the pan. As soon as they are cool enough to handle, remove the shells and legs, leaving the tails intact.

4 In a large saucepan, heat the remaining olive oil and fry the shallots and garlic for 3–4 minutes over a gentle heat until the shallots are soft but not brown. Add the rice and cook for a few minutes, stirring, until the rice is coated with oil and the grains are slightly translucent. Stir in the tomatoes, with the reserved liquid from the mussels.

5 When all the free liquid has been absorbed, add the remaining wine, stirring constantly. When it has also been absorbed, gradually add the hot stock, one ladleful at a time, continuing to stir the rice constantly and waiting until each quantity of stock has been absorbed before adding the next.

6 When the risotto is three-quarters cooked, carefully stir in all the seafood, except the mussels reserved for the garnish. Continue to cook until all the stock has been absorbed and the rice is tender but still has a bit of "bite".

7 Stir in the parsley and cream and adjust the seasoning. Cover the pan and leave the risotto to stand for 2–3 minutes. Serve in individual bowls, garnished with the reserved mussels in their shells.

CHAMPAGNE RISOTTO

THIS MAY SEEM RATHER EXTRAVAGANT, BUT IT MAKES A REALLY BEAUTIFULLY FLAVOURED RISOTTO, PERFECT FOR THAT SPECIAL ANNIVERSARY DINNER.

SERVES THREE TO FOUR

INGREDIENTS

25g/1oz/2 tbsp butter
2 shallots, finely chopped
275g/10oz/1½ cups risotto rice,
  preferably Carnaroli
½ bottle or 300ml/½ pint/1¼ cups
  champagne
750ml/1¼ pints/3 cups simmering
  light vegetable or chicken stock
150ml/¼ pint/⅔ cup double cream
40g/1½oz/½ cup freshly grated
  Parmesan cheese
10ml/2 tsp very finely chopped fresh
  chervil
salt and freshly ground black pepper
black truffle shavings, to garnish
  (optional)

1 Melt the butter in a pan and fry the shallots for 2–3 minutes until softened. Add the rice and cook, stirring all the time, until the grains are evenly coated in butter and are beginning to look translucent around the edges.

2 Pour in about two-thirds of the champagne and cook over a high heat so that the liquid bubbles fiercely. Cook, stirring, until all the liquid has been absorbed before beginning to add the hot stock.

3 Add the stock, a ladleful at a time, making sure that each addition has been completely absorbed before adding the next. The risotto should gradually become creamy and velvety and all the stock should be absorbed.

4 When the rice is tender but retains a bit of "bite", stir in the remaining champagne and the double cream and Parmesan. Adjust the seasoning. Remove from the heat, cover and leave to stand for a few minutes. Stir in the chervil. If you want to gild the lily, garnish with a few truffle shavings.

ROASTED PEPPER RISOTTO

THIS MAKES AN EXCELLENT VEGETARIAN SUPPER DISH, OR A STARTER FOR SIX.

<u>SERVES THREE TO FOUR</u>

INGREDIENTS
1 red pepper
1 yellow pepper
15ml/1 tbsp olive oil
25g/1oz/2 tbsp butter
1 onion, chopped
2 garlic cloves, crushed
275g/10oz/1½ cups risotto rice
1 litre/1¾ pints/4 cups simmering
  vegetable stock
50g/2oz/⅔ cup freshly grated
  Parmesan cheese
salt and freshly ground black pepper
freshly grated Parmesan cheese, to
  serve (optional)

1 Preheat the grill to high. Cut the peppers in half, remove the seeds and pith and arrange, cut side down, on a baking sheet. Place under the grill for 5–6 minutes until the skin is charred. Put the peppers in a plastic bag, tie the ends and leave for 4–5 minutes.

2 Peel the peppers when they are cool enough to handle and the steam has loosened the skin. Cut into thin strips.

3 Heat the oil and butter in a pan and fry the onion and garlic for 4–5 minutes over a low heat until the onion begins to soften. Add the peppers and cook the mixture for 3–4 minutes more, stirring occasionally.

4 Stir in the rice. Cook over a medium heat for 3–4 minutes, stirring all the time, until the rice is evenly coated in oil and the outer part of each grain has become translucent.

5 Add a ladleful of stock. Cook, stirring, until all the liquid has been absorbed. Continue to add the stock, a ladleful at a time, making sure each quantity has been absorbed before adding the next.

6 When the rice is tender but retains a bit of "bite", stir in the Parmesan, and add seasoning to taste. Cover and leave to stand for 3–4 minutes, then serve, with extra Parmesan, if using.

Two Cheese Risotto

This undeniably rich and creamy risotto is just the thing to serve on cold winter evenings when everyone needs warming up.

SERVES THREE TO FOUR

INGREDIENTS
7.5ml/1½ tsp olive oil
50g/2oz/4 tbsp butter
1 onion, finely chopped
1 garlic clove, crushed
275g/10oz/1½ cups risotto rice,
   preferably Vialone Nano
175ml/6fl oz/¾ cup dry white wine
1 litre/1¾ pints/4 cups simmering
   vegetable or chicken stock
75g/3oz/¾ cup fontina cheese, cubed
50g/2oz/⅔ cup freshly grated
   Parmesan cheese, plus extra, to
   serve
salt and freshly ground black pepper

1 Heat the olive oil with half the butter in a pan and gently fry the onion and garlic for 5–6 minutes until soft. Add the rice and cook, stirring all the time, until the grains are coated in fat and have become slightly translucent around the edges.

2 Stir in the wine. Cook, stirring, until the liquid has been absorbed, then add a ladleful of hot stock. Stir until the stock has been absorbed, then add the remaining stock in the same way, waiting for each quantity of stock to be absorbed before adding more.

3 When the rice is half cooked, stir in the fontina cheese, and continue cooking and adding stock. Keep stirring the rice all the time.

4 When the risotto is creamy and the grains are tender but still have a bit of "bite", stir in the remaining butter and the Parmesan. Season, then remove the pan from the heat, cover and leave to rest for 3–4 minutes before serving.

Quick Risotto

This is rather a cheat's risotto as it defies all the rules that insist the stock is added gradually. Instead, the rice is cooked quickly in a conventional way, and the other ingredients are simply thrown in at the last minute. It tastes good for all that.

SERVES THREE TO FOUR

INGREDIENTS
275g/10oz/1½ cups risotto rice
1 litre/1¾ pints/4 cups simmering
   chicken stock
115g/4oz/1 cup mozzarella cheese,
   cut into small cubes
2 egg yolks
30ml/2 tbsp freshly grated Parmesan
   cheese
75g/3oz cooked ham, cut into small
   cubes
30ml/2 tbsp chopped fresh parsley
salt and freshly ground black pepper
fresh parsley sprigs, to garnish
freshly grated Parmesan cheese, to
   serve

1 Put the rice in a pan. Pour in the stock, bring to the boil and then cover and simmer for about 18–20 minutes until the rice is tender.

2 Remove the pan from the heat and quickly stir in the mozzarella, egg yolks, Parmesan, ham and parsley. Season well with salt and pepper.

3 Cover the pan and stand for 2–3 minutes to allow the cheese to melt, then stir again. Pile into warmed serving bowls and serve immediately, with extra Parmesan cheese.

PESTO RISOTTO

IF YOU BUY THE PESTO — AND THERE ARE SOME GOOD VARIETIES AVAILABLE NOWADAYS — THIS IS JUST ABOUT AS EASY AS A RISOTTO GETS.

SERVES THREE TO FOUR

INGREDIENTS
   30ml/2 tbsp olive oil
   2 shallots, finely chopped
   1 garlic clove, crushed
   275g/10oz/1½ cups risotto rice
   175ml/6fl oz/¾ cup dry white wine
   1 litre/1¾ pints/4 cups simmering
      vegetable stock
   45ml/3 tbsp pesto
   25g/1oz/⅓ cup freshly grated
      Parmesan cheese, plus extra, to
      serve (optional)
   salt and freshly ground black pepper

1 Heat the olive oil in a pan and fry the shallots and garlic for 4–5 minutes until the shallots are soft but not browned.

2 Add the rice and cook over a medium heat, stirring all the time, until the grains of rice are coated in oil and the outer part of the grain is translucent and the inner part opaque.

3 Pour in the wine. Cook, stirring, until all of it has been absorbed, then start adding the hot stock, a ladleful at a time, stirring constantly and waiting until each addition of stock has been absorbed before adding the next.

4 After about 20 minutes, when all the stock has been absorbed and the rice is creamy and tender, stir in the pesto and Parmesan. Taste and adjust seasoning and then cover and rest for 3–4 minutes. Spoon into a bowl and serve, with extra Parmesan, if you like.

PUMPKIN AND APPLE RISOTTO

PUMPKIN AND OTHER WINTER SQUASH ARE VERY POPULAR IN ITALY AND APPEAR IN MANY CLASSIC RECIPES. IF PUMPKINS ARE OUT OF SEASON, USE BUTTERNUT OR ONION SQUASH — THE FLAVOURS WILL BE SLIGHTLY DIFFERENT, BUT THEY BOTH WORK WELL.

SERVES THREE TO FOUR

INGREDIENTS
   225g/8oz butternut squash or
      pumpkin flesh
   1 cooking apple
   120ml/4fl oz/½ cup water
   25g/1oz/2 tbsp butter
   25ml/1½ tbsp olive oil
   1 onion, finely chopped
   1 garlic clove, crushed
   275g/10oz/1½ cups risotto rice, such
      as Vialone Nano
   175ml/6fl oz/¾ cup fruity white wine
   900ml–1 litre/1½–1¾ pints/3¾–4
      cups simmering vegetable stock
   75g/3oz/1 cup freshly grated
      Parmesan cheese
   salt and freshly ground black pepper

1 Cut the squash into small pieces. Peel, core and roughly chop the apple. Place in a pan and pour in the water. Bring to the boil, then simmer for about 15–20 minutes until the squash is very tender. Drain, return the squash mixture to the pan and add half the butter. Mash the mixture roughly with a fork to break up any large pieces, but leave the mixture chunky.

2 Heat the oil and remaining butter in a pan and fry the onion and garlic until the onion is soft. Tip in the rice. Cook, stirring constantly, over a medium heat for 2 minutes until it is coated in oil and the grains are slightly translucent.

3 Add the wine and stir into the rice. When all the liquid has been absorbed, begin to add the stock a ladleful at a time, making sure each addition has been absorbed before adding the next. This should take about 20 minutes.

4 When roughly two ladlefuls of stock are left, add the squash and apple mixture together with another addition of stock. Continue to cook, stirring well and adding the rest of the stock, until the risotto is very creamy. Stir in the Parmesan cheese, adjust the seasoning and serve immediately.

ROSEMARY RISOTTO WITH BORLOTTI BEANS

THIS IS A CLASSIC RISOTTO WITH A SUBTLE AND COMPLEX TASTE, FROM THE HEADY FLAVOURS OF ROSEMARY TO THE SAVOURY BEANS AND THE FRUITY-SWEET FLAVOURS OF MASCARPONE AND PARMESAN.

SERVES THREE TO FOUR

INGREDIENTS
400g/14oz can borlotti beans
30ml/2 tbsp olive oil
1 onion, chopped
2 garlic cloves, crushed
275g/10oz/1½ cups risotto rice
175ml/6fl oz/¾ cup dry white wine
900ml–1 litre/1½–1¾ pints/
  3¾–4 cups simmering vegetable or
  chicken stock
60ml/4 tbsp mascarpone cheese
65g/2½oz/scant 1 cup freshly grated
  Parmesan cheese, plus extra, to
  serve (optional)
5ml/1 tsp chopped fresh rosemary
salt and freshly ground black pepper

1 Drain the beans, rinse under cold water and drain again. Purée about two-thirds of the beans fairly coarsely in a food processor or blender. Set the remaining beans aside.

2 Heat the olive oil in a large pan and gently fry the onion and garlic for 6–8 minutes until very soft. Add the rice and cook over a medium heat for a few minutes, stirring constantly, until the grains are thoroughly coated in oil and are slightly translucent.

VARIATION
Fresh thyme or marjoram could be used for this risotto instead of rosemary, if preferred. One of the great virtues of risotto is that it lends itself well to variations. Experiment with different herbs to make your own speciality dish.

3 Pour in the wine. Cook over a medium heat for 2–3 minutes, stirring all the time, until the wine has been absorbed. Add the stock gradually, a ladleful at a time, waiting for each quantity to be absorbed before adding more, and continuing to stir.

4 When the rice is three-quarters cooked, stir in the bean purée. Continue to cook the risotto, adding the remaining stock, until it is creamy and the rice is tender but still has a bit of "bite". Add the reserved beans, with the mascarpone, Parmesan and rosemary, then season to taste. Stir thoroughly, then cover and leave to stand for about 5 minutes so that the risotto absorbs the flavours fully and the rice completes cooking. Serve with extra Parmesan, if you like.

JERUSALEM ARTICHOKE RISOTTO

THIS IS A SIMPLE AND WARMING RISOTTO, WHICH BENEFITS FROM THE DELICIOUS AND DISTINCTIVE FLAVOUR OF JERUSALEM ARTICHOKES.

SERVES THREE TO FOUR

INGREDIENTS

400g/14oz Jerusalem artichokes
40g/1½oz/3 tbsp butter
15ml/1 tbsp olive oil
1 onion, finely chopped
1 garlic clove, crushed
275g/10oz/1½ cups risotto rice
120ml/4fl oz/½ cup fruity white wine
1 litre/1¾ pints/4 cups simmering
  vegetable stock
10ml/2 tsp chopped fresh thyme
40g/1½oz/½ cup freshly grated
  Parmesan cheese, plus extra, to
  serve
salt and freshly ground black pepper
fresh thyme sprigs, to garnish

1 Peel the artichokes, cut them into pieces and immediately add them to a pan of lightly salted water. Simmer them until tender, then drain and mash with 15g/½oz/1 tbsp of the butter. Add a little more salt, if needed.

2 Heat the oil and the remaining butter in a pan and fry the onion and garlic for 5–6 minutes until soft. Add the rice and cook over a medium heat for about 2 minutes until the grains are translucent around the edges.

3 Pour in the wine, stir until it has been absorbed, then start adding the simmering stock, a ladleful at a time, making sure each quantity has been absorbed before adding more.

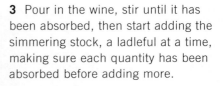

4 When you have just one last ladleful of stock to add, stir in the mashed artichokes and the chopped thyme. Season with salt and pepper. Continue cooking until the risotto is creamy and the artichokes are hot. Stir in the Parmesan. Remove from the heat, cover the pan and leave the risotto to stand for a few minutes. Spoon into a serving dish, garnish with thyme, and serve with Parmesan cheese.

DUCK RISOTTO

THIS MAKES AN EXCELLENT STARTER FOR SIX OR COULD BE SERVED FOR HALF THAT NUMBER AS A LUNCH OR SUPPER DISH. ADD A GREEN SALAD, OR SERVE WITH MANGETOUTS AND SAUTÉED RED PEPPER SLICES.

SERVES THREE TO FOUR

INGREDIENTS
2 duck breasts
30ml/2 tbsp brandy
30ml/2 tbsp orange juice
15ml/1 tbsp olive oil (optional)
1 onion, finely chopped
1 garlic clove, crushed
275g/10oz/1½ cups risotto rice
1–1.2 litres/1¾–2 pints/4–5 cups
  simmering duck, turkey or chicken
  stock
5ml/1 tsp chopped fresh thyme
5ml/1 tsp chopped fresh mint
10ml/2 tsp grated orange rind
40g/1½oz/½ cup freshly grated
  Parmesan cheese
salt and freshly ground black pepper
strips of thinly pared orange rind, to
  garnish

1 Score the fatty side of the duck breasts and rub them with salt. Put them, fat side down, in a heavy frying pan and dry-fry over a medium heat for 6–8 minutes to render the fat. Transfer the breasts to a plate and then pull away and discard the fat. Cut the flesh into strips about 2cm/¾in wide.

2 Pour all but 15ml/1 tbsp of the rendered duck fat from the pan into a cup or jug, then reheat the fat in the pan. Fry the duck slices for 2–3 minutes over a medium high heat until evenly brown but not overcooked. Add the brandy, heat to simmering point and then ignite, either by tilting the pan or using a taper. When the flames have died down, add the orange juice and season with salt and pepper. Remove from the heat and set aside.

3 In a saucepan, heat either 15ml/ 1 tbsp of the remaining duck fat or use olive oil. Fry the onion and garlic over a gentle heat until the onion is soft but not browned. Add the rice and cook, stirring all the time, until the grains are coated in oil and have become slightly translucent around the edges.

4 Add the stock, a ladleful at a time, waiting for each quantity of stock to be absorbed completely before adding the next. Just before adding the final ladleful of stock, stir in the duck, with the thyme and mint. Continue cooking until the risotto is creamy and the rice is tender but still has a bit of "bite".

5 Add the orange rind and Parmesan. Taste and adjust the seasoning, then remove from the heat, cover the pan and leave to stand for a few minutes. Serve on individual plates, garnished with the pared orange rind.

CHICKEN LIVER RISOTTO

THE COMBINATION OF CHICKEN LIVERS, BACON, PARSLEY AND THYME GIVES THIS RISOTTO A WONDERFULLY RICH FLAVOUR. SERVE IT AS A STARTER FOR FOUR OR A LUNCH FOR TWO OR THREE.

SERVES TWO TO FOUR

INGREDIENTS
175g/6oz chicken livers
about 15ml/1 tbsp olive oil
about 25g/1oz/2 tbsp butter
about 40g/1½oz speck or 3 rindless
   streaky bacon rashers, finely
   chopped
2 shallots, finely chopped
1 garlic clove, crushed
1 celery stick, finely sliced
275g/10oz/1½ cups risotto rice
175ml/6fl oz/¾ cup dry white wine
900ml–1 litre/1½–1¾ pints/3¾–4
   cups simmering chicken stock
5ml/1 tsp chopped fresh thyme
15ml/1 tbsp chopped fresh parsley
salt and freshly ground black pepper
parsley and thyme sprigs to garnish

1 Clean the chicken livers carefully, removing any fat or membrane. Rinse well, pat dry with kitchen paper and cut into small, even pieces.

2 Heat the oil and butter in a frying pan and fry the speck or bacon for 2–3 minutes. Add the shallots, garlic and celery and continue frying for 3–4 minutes over a low heat until the vegetables are slightly softened. Increase the heat and add the chicken livers, stir-frying for a few minutes until they are brown all over.

3 Add the rice. Cook, stirring, for a few minutes, then pour over the wine. Allow to boil so that the alcohol is driven off. Stir frequently, taking care not to break up the chicken livers. When all the wine has been absorbed, add the hot stock, a ladleful at a time, stirring constantly.

4 About halfway through cooking, add the thyme and season with salt and pepper. Continue to add the stock as before, making sure that each quantity has been absorbed before adding more.

5 When the risotto is creamy and the rice is tender but still has a bit of "bite", stir in the parsley. Taste and adjust the seasoning. Remove the pan from the heat, cover and leave to rest for a few minutes before serving, garnished with parsley and thyme.

LEEK AND HAM RISOTTO

ANOTHER SIMPLE RISOTTO THAT MAKES AN EASY SUPPER, YET IS SPECIAL ENOUGH FOR A DINNER PARTY.

SERVES THREE TO FOUR

INGREDIENTS
  7.5ml/1½ tsp olive oil
  40g/1½oz/3 tbsp butter
  2 leeks, cut in slices
  175g/6oz prosciutto, torn into pieces
  75g/3oz/generous 1 cup button
    mushrooms, sliced
  275g/10oz/1½ cups risotto rice
  1 litre/1¾ pints/4 cups simmering
    chicken stock
  45ml/3 tbsp chopped fresh flat leaf
    parsley
  40g/1½oz/½ cup freshly grated
    Parmesan cheese
  salt and freshly ground black pepper

1 Heat the oil and butter in a pan and fry the leeks until soft. Set aside a few strips of prosciutto for the garnish and add the rest to the pan. Fry for 1 minute, then add the mushrooms and stir-fry for 2–3 minutes until lightly browned.

2 Add the rice. Cook, stirring, for 1–2 minutes until the grains are evenly coated in oil and have become translucent around the edges. Add a ladleful of hot stock. Stir until this has been absorbed completely, then add the next ladleful. Continue in this way until all the stock has been absorbed.

3 When the risotto is creamy and the rice is tender but still has a bit of "bite", stir in the parsley and Parmesan. Adjust the seasoning, remove from the heat and cover. Allow to rest for a few minutes. Spoon into a bowl, garnish with the reserved prosciutto and serve.

RABBIT AND LEMON GRASS RISOTTO

THE LEMON GRASS ADDS A PLEASANT TANG TO THIS RISOTTO. IF RABBIT ISN'T AVAILABLE, USE CHICKEN OR TURKEY INSTEAD.

SERVES THREE TO FOUR

INGREDIENTS
  225g/8oz rabbit meat, cut into strips
  seasoned flour
  50g/2oz/¼ cup butter
  15ml/1 tbsp olive oil
  45ml/3 tbsp dry sherry
  1 onion, finely chopped
  1 garlic clove, crushed
  1 lemon grass stalk, peeled and very
    finely sliced
  275g/10oz/1½ cups risotto rice,
    preferably Carnaroli
  1 litre/1¾ pints/4 cups simmering
    chicken stock
  10ml/2 tsp chopped fresh thyme
  45ml/3 tbsp double cream
  25g/1oz/⅓ cup freshly grated
    Parmesan cheese
  salt and freshly ground black pepper

1 Coat the rabbit strips in the seasoned flour. Heat half the butter and olive oil in a frying pan and fry the rabbit quickly until evenly brown. Add the sherry, and allow to boil briefly to burn off the alcohol. Season with salt and pepper and set aside.

2 Heat the remaining olive oil and butter in a large saucepan. Fry the onion and garlic over a low heat for 4–5 minutes until the onion is soft. Add the sliced lemon grass and cook for a few more minutes.

3 Add the rice and stir to coat in the oil. Add a ladleful of stock and cook, stirring, until the liquid has been absorbed. Continue adding the stock gradually, stirring constantly. When the rice is almost cooked, stir in three-quarters of the rabbit strips, with the pan juices. Add the thyme and seasoning.

4 Continue cooking until the rice is tender but still has a "bite". Stir in the cream and Parmesan, remove from the heat and cover. Leave to rest before serving, garnished with rabbit strips.

APPLE AND LEMON RISOTTO WITH POACHED PLUMS

ALTHOUGH IT'S ENTIRELY POSSIBLE TO COOK THIS BY THE CONVENTIONAL RISOTTO METHOD — BY ADDING THE LIQUID SLOWLY — IT MAKES MORE SENSE TO COOK THE RICE WITH THE MILK, IN THE SAME WAY AS FOR A RICE PUDDING.

SERVES FOUR

INGREDIENTS
  1 cooking apple
  15g/½oz/1 tbsp butter
  175g/6oz/scant 1 cup risotto rice
  600ml/1 pint/2½ cups creamy milk
  about 50g/2oz/¼ cup caster sugar
  1.5ml/¼ tsp ground cinnamon
  30ml/2 tbsp lemon juice
  45ml/3 tbsp double cream
  grated rind of 1 lemon, to decorate
For the poached plums
  50g/2oz/¼ cup light brown
    muscovado sugar
  200ml/7fl oz/scant 1 cup apple juice
  3 star anise
  cinnamon stick
  6 plums, halved and sliced

1 Peel and core the apple. Cut it into large chunks. Put these in a large, non-stick pan and add the butter. Heat gently until the butter melts.

2 Add the rice and milk and stir well. Bring to the boil over a medium heat, then simmer very gently for 20–25 minutes, stirring occasionally.

COOK'S TIP
If the apple is very sharp (acidic) the milk may curdle. There is no need to worry about this – it won't affect the look or taste of the sauce.

3 To make the poached plums, dissolve the sugar in 150ml/¼ pints/⅔ cup apple juice in a pan. Add the spices and bring to the boil. Boil for 2 minutes. Add the plums, and simmer for 2 minutes. Set aside until ready to serve.

4 Stir the sugar, cinnamon and lemon juice into the risotto. Cook for 2 minutes, stirring all the time, then stir in the cream. Taste and add more sugar if necessary. Decorate with the lemon rind and serve with the poached plums.

CHOCOLATE RISOTTO

IF YOU'VE NEVER TASTED A SWEET RISOTTO, THERE'S A TREAT IN STORE. CHOCOLATE RISOTTO IS DELECTABLE, AND CHILDREN OF ALL AGES LOVE IT.

SERVES FOUR TO SIX

INGREDIENTS
   175g/6oz/scant 1 cup risotto rice
   600ml/1 pint/2½ cups creamy milk
   75g/3oz plain chocolate, broken into
     pieces
   25g/1oz/2 tbsp butter
   about 50g/2oz/¼ cup caster sugar
   pinch of ground cinnamon
   60ml/4 tbsp double cream
   fresh raspberries and chocolate
     caraque, to decorate
   chocolate sauce, to serve

3 Remove the pan from the heat and stir in the ground cinnamon and double cream. Cover the pan and leave to stand for a few minutes.

4 Spoon the risotto into individual dishes or dessert plates, and decorate with fresh raspberries and chocolate caraque. Serve with chocolate sauce.

1 Put the rice in a non-stick pan. Pour in the milk and bring to the boil over a low to medium heat. Reduce the heat to the lowest setting and simmer very gently for about 20 minutes, stirring occasionally, until the rice is very soft.

2 Stir in the chocolate, butter and sugar. Cook, stirring all the time over a very gentle heat for 1–2 minutes, until the chocolate has melted.

CHICKEN BIRYANI

EASY TO MAKE AND VERY TASTY, THIS CLASSIC INDIAN DISH IS IDEAL FOR A SIMPLE SUPPER.

SERVES FOUR

INGREDIENTS
  10 whole green cardamom pods
  275g/10oz/1½ cups basmati rice,
    soaked and drained
  2.5ml/½ tsp salt
  2–3 whole cloves
  5cm/2in cinnamon stick
  45ml/3 tbsp vegetable oil
  3 onions, sliced
  4 chicken breasts, each about
    175g/6oz, cubed
  1.5ml/¼ tsp ground cloves
  1.5ml/¼ tsp hot chilli powder
  5ml/1 tsp ground cumin
  5ml/1 tsp ground coriander
  2.5ml/½ tsp ground black pepper
  3 garlic cloves, chopped
  5ml/1 tsp finely chopped fresh
    root ginger
  juice of 1 lemon
  4 tomatoes, sliced
  30ml/2 tbsp chopped fresh coriander
  150ml/¼ pint/⅔ cup natural yogurt
  4–5 saffron strands, soaked in
    10ml/2 tsp hot milk
  150ml/¼ pint/⅔ cup water
  toasted flaked almonds and fresh
    coriander sprigs, to garnish
  natural yogurt, to serve

1 Preheat the oven to 190°C/375°F/ Gas 5. Remove the seeds from half the cardamom pods and grind them finely, using a pestle and mortar. Set them aside. Bring a pan of water to the boil and add the rice, salt, whole cardamom pods, cloves and cinnamon stick. Boil for 2 minutes, then drain, leaving the whole spices in the rice.

2 Heat the oil in a frying pan and fry the onions for 8 minutes, until softened and browned. Add the chicken and the ground spices, including the ground cardamom seeds. Mix well, then add the garlic, ginger and lemon juice. Stir-fry for 5 minutes.

3 Transfer the chicken mixture to a casserole and arrange the tomatoes on top. Sprinkle on the fresh coriander, spoon the yogurt evenly on top and cover with the drained rice.

4 Drizzle the saffron milk over the rice and pour over the water. Cover tightly and bake for 1 hour. Transfer to a warmed serving platter and remove the whole spices from the rice. Garnish with toasted almonds and fresh coriander sprigs and serve with the natural yogurt.

BASMATI AND NUT PILAFF

VEGETARIANS WILL LOVE THIS SIMPLE PILAFF. ADD WILD OR CULTIVATED MUSHROOMS, IF YOU LIKE.

SERVES FOUR

INGREDIENTS

15–30ml/1–2 tbsp sunflower oil
1 onion, chopped
1 garlic clove, crushed
1 large carrot, coarsely grated
225g/8oz/generous 1 cup basmati
  rice, soaked
5ml/1 tsp cumin seeds
10ml/2 tsp ground coriander
10ml/2 tsp black mustard seeds
  (optional)
4 green cardamom pods
450ml/¾ pint/scant 2 cups vegetable
  stock or water
1 bay leaf
75g/3oz/¾ cup unsalted walnuts and
  cashew nuts
salt and freshly ground black pepper
fresh parsley or coriander sprigs,
  to garnish

1 Heat the oil in a large, shallow frying pan and gently fry the onion, garlic and carrot for 3–4 minutes. Drain the rice and then add to the pan with the spices. Cook for 1–2 minutes more, stirring to coat the grains in oil.

2 Pour in the stock or water, add the bay leaf and season well. Bring to the boil, lower the heat, cover and simmer very gently for 10–12 minutes.

3 Remove the pan from the heat without lifting the lid. Leave to stand for about 5 minutes, then check the rice. If it is cooked, there will be small steam holes on the surface of the rice. Remove and discard the bay leaf and the cardamom pods.

4 Stir in the nuts and check the seasoning. Spoon on to a platter, garnish with the parsley or coriander and serve.

COOK'S TIP
Use whichever nuts you prefer in this dish – even unsalted peanuts taste good, although almonds, cashew nuts or pistachios are more exotic.

LAMB PARSI

THIS IS SIMILAR TO BIRYANI, BUT HERE THE LAMB IS MARINATED WITH THE YOGURT, A TECHNIQUE WHICH IS A PARSI SPECIALITY. SERVE WITH A DHAL OR WITH SPICED MUSHROOMS.

SERVES SIX

INGREDIENTS
900g/2lb lamb fillet, cut into
2.5cm/1in cubes
60ml/4 tbsp ghee or butter
2 onions, sliced
450g/1lb potatoes, cut into large
chunks
chicken stock or water (see method)
450g/1lb/2⅓ cups basmati rice,
soaked
generous pinch of saffron strands,
dissolved in 30ml/2 tbsp warm milk
fresh coriander sprigs, to garnish
For the marinade
475ml/16fl oz/2 cups natural yogurt
3–4 garlic cloves, crushed
10ml/2 tsp cayenne pepper
20ml/4 tsp garam masala
10ml/2 tsp ground cumin
5ml/1 tsp ground coriander

1 Make the marinade by mixing all the ingredients in a large bowl. Add the meat, stir to coat, then cover and leave to marinate for 3–4 hours in a cool place or overnight in the fridge.

2 Melt 30ml/2 tbsp of the ghee or butter in a large saucepan and fry the onions for 6–8 minutes until lightly golden. Transfer to a plate.

3 Melt a further 25ml/1½ tbsp of the ghee or butter in the pan. Fry the marinated lamb cubes in batches until evenly brown, transferring each batch in turn to a plate. When all the lamb has been browned, return it to the pan and scrape in the remaining marinade.

4 Stir in the potatoes and add about three-quarters of the fried onions. Pour in just enough chicken stock or water to cover the mixture. Bring to the boil, then cover and simmer over a very low heat for 40–50 minutes until the lamb is tender and the potatoes are cooked. Preheat the oven to 160°C/325°F/Gas 3.

5 Drain the rice. Cook it in a pan of boiling stock or water for 5 minutes. Meanwhile, spoon the lamb mixture into a casserole. Drain the rice and mound it on top of the lamb, then, using the handle of a wooden spoon, make a hole down the centre. Top with the remaining fried onions, pour the saffron milk over the top and dot with the remaining ghee or butter.

6 Cover the pan with a double layer of foil and a lid. Cook in the oven for 30–35 minutes or until the rice is completely tender. Garnish with fresh coriander sprigs and serve.

COOK'S TIP
Take care not to overcook the rice when parboiling it. The grains should still be quite hard, but should have a slightly powdery consistency.

INDIAN RICE WITH TOMATOES AND SPINACH

THIS TASTY RICE DISH CAN BE SERVED WITH A MEAT CURRY OR AS PART OF A VEGETARIAN MEAL.

SERVES FOUR

INGREDIENTS
    30ml/2 tbsp sunflower oil
    15ml/1 tbsp ghee or butter
    1 onion, chopped
    2 garlic cloves, crushed
    3 tomatoes, peeled, seeded and
      chopped
    225g/8oz/generous 1 cup brown
      basmati rice, soaked
    10ml/2 tsp dhana jeera powder or
      5ml/1 tsp ground coriander and
      5ml/1 tsp ground cumin
    2 carrots, coarsely grated
    900ml/1½ pints/3¾ cups vegetable
      stock
    275g/10oz baby spinach leaves,
      washed
    50g/2oz/½ cup unsalted cashew nuts,
      toasted
    salt and freshly ground black pepper

1 Heat the oil and ghee or butter in a flameproof casserole and gently fry the onion and garlic for 4–5 minutes until soft. Add the chopped tomatoes and cook for 3–4 minutes, stirring, until slightly thickened.

2 Drain the rice, add it to the casserole and cook gently for 1–2 minutes, stirring, until the rice is coated with the tomato and onion mixture.

3 Stir in the dhana jeera powder or coriander and cumin, then add the carrots and season with salt and pepper. Pour in the stock and stir well to mix.

4 Bring to the boil, then cover tightly and simmer over a very gentle heat for 20–25 minutes until the rice is tender. Lay the spinach on the surface of the rice, cover again and cook for 2–3 minutes until the spinach has wilted. Fold the spinach into the rest of the rice and check the seasoning. Sprinkle with cashews and serve.

COOK'S TIP
If you can't get baby spinach leaves, use larger fresh spinach leaves. Remove any tough stalks and chop the leaves roughly.

PILAU RICE WITH WHOLE SPICES

THIS FRAGRANT RICE DISH MAKES A PERFECT ACCOMPANIMENT TO ANY INDIAN MEAL.

SERVES FOUR

INGREDIENTS
generous pinch of saffron
  strands
600ml/1 pint/2½ cups hot
  chicken stock
50g/2oz/¼ cup butter
1 onion, chopped
1 garlic clove, crushed
½ cinnamon stick
6 green cardamom pods
1 bay leaf
250g/9oz/1⅓ cups basmati rice
50g/2oz/⅓ cup sultanas
15ml/1 tbsp sunflower oil
50g/2oz/½ cup cashew nuts
naan bread and tomato and onion
  salad, to serve (optional)

1 Stir the saffron strands into a jug of hot stock and set aside.

2 Heat the butter in a saucepan and fry the onion and garlic for 5 minutes. Stir in the cinnamon stick, cardamoms and bay leaf and cook for 2 minutes.

3 Add the rice and cook, stirring, for 2 minutes more. Pour in the saffron-flavoured stock and add the sultanas. Bring to the boil, stir, then lower the heat, cover and cook gently for about 10 minutes or until the rice is tender and the liquid has all been absorbed.

4 Meanwhile, heat the oil in a frying pan and fry the cashew nuts until browned. Drain on kitchen paper. Scatter the cashew nuts over the rice. Serve with naan bread and a tomato and onion salad, if you like.

COOK'S TIP
Don't be tempted to use black cardamoms in this dish. They are coarser and more strongly flavoured than green cardamoms and are only used in highly spiced dishes that are cooked for a long time.

MUSHROOM PILAU

THIS DISH IS SIMPLICITY ITSELF. SERVE WITH ANY INDIAN DISH OR WITH ROAST LAMB OR CHICKEN.

SERVES FOUR

INGREDIENTS
  30ml/2 tbsp vegetable oil
  2 shallots, finely chopped
  1 garlic clove, crushed
  3 green cardamom pods
  25g/1oz/2 tbsp ghee or butter
  175g/6oz/2½ cups button
    mushrooms, sliced
  225g/8oz/generous 1 cup basmati
    rice, soaked
  5ml/1 tsp grated fresh root ginger
  good pinch of garam masala
  450ml/¾ pint/scant 2 cups water
  15ml/1 tbsp chopped fresh coriander
  salt

1 Heat the oil in a flameproof casserole and fry the shallots, garlic and cardamom pods over a medium heat for 3–4 minutes until the shallots have softened and are beginning to brown.

2 Add the ghee or butter. When it has melted, add the mushrooms and fry for 2–3 minutes more.

3 Add the rice, ginger and garam masala. Stir-fry over a low heat for 2–3 minutes, then stir in the water and a little salt. Bring to the boil, then cover tightly and simmer over a very low heat for 10 minutes.

4 Remove the casserole from the heat. Leave to stand, covered, for 5 minutes. Add the chopped coriander and fork it through the rice. Spoon into a serving bowl and serve at once.

CHICKEN AND MUSHROOM DONBURI

"DONBURI" MEANS A ONE-DISH MEAL THAT IS EATEN FROM A BOWL, AND TAKES ITS NAME FROM THE EPONYMOUS JAPANESE PORCELAIN FOOD BOWL. AS IN MOST JAPANESE DISHES, THE RICE HERE IS COMPLETELY PLAIN BUT IS NEVERTHELESS AN INTEGRAL PART OF THE DISH.

SERVES FOUR

INGREDIENTS
   10ml/2 tsp groundnut oil
   50g/2oz/4 tbsp butter
   2 garlic cloves, crushed
   2.5cm/1in piece of fresh root ginger,
    grated
   5 spring onions, diagonally sliced
   1 green fresh chilli, seeded and
    finely sliced
   3 skinless, boneless chicken breasts,
    cut into thin strips
   150g/5oz tofu, cut into small cubes
   115g/4oz/1¾ shiitake mushrooms,
    stalks discarded and cups sliced
   15ml/1 tbsp Japanese rice wine
   30ml/2 tbsp light soy sauce
   10ml/2 tsp granulated sugar
   400ml/14fl oz/1⅔ cups chicken stock
For the rice
   225–275g/8–10oz/generous
    1–1½ cups Japanese rice or Thai
    fragrant rice

1 Cook the rice by the absorption method or by following the instructions on the packet.

2 While the rice is cooking, heat the oil and half the butter in a large frying pan. Stir-fry the garlic, ginger, spring onions and chilli for 1–2 minutes until slightly softened. Add the strips of chicken and fry, in batches if necessary, until all the pieces are evenly browned.

3 Transfer the chicken mixture to a plate and add the tofu to the pan. Stir-fry for a few minutes, then add the mushrooms. Stir-fry for 2–3 minutes over a medium heat until the mushrooms are tender.

4 Stir in the rice wine, soy sauce and sugar and cook briskly for 1–2 minutes, stirring all the time. Return the chicken to the pan, toss over the heat for about 2 minutes, then pour in the stock. Stir well and cook over a gentle heat for 5–6 minutes until bubbling.

5 Spoon the rice into individual serving bowls and pile the chicken mixture on top, making sure that each portion gets a generous amount of chicken sauce.

COOK'S TIP
Once the rice is cooked, leave it covered until ready to serve. It will stay warm for about 30 minutes. Fork through lightly just before serving.

CHINESE FRIED RICE

THIS DISH, A VARIATION ON SPECIAL FRIED RICE, IS MORE ELABORATE THAN THE MORE FAMILIAR EGG FRIED RICE, AND IS A MEAL IN ITSELF.

SERVES FOUR

INGREDIENTS
    50g/2oz cooked ham
    50g/2oz cooked prawns, peeled
    3 eggs
    5ml/1 tsp salt
    2 spring onions, finely chopped
    60ml/4 tbsp vegetable oil
    115g/4oz/1 cup green peas, thawed
        if frozen
    15ml/1 tbsp light soy sauce
    15ml/1 tbsp Chinese rice wine or dry
        sherry
    450g/1lb/4 cups cooked white long
        grain rice

1 Dice the cooked ham finely. Pat the cooked prawns dry on kitchen paper.

2 In a bowl, beat the eggs with a pinch of salt and a few spring onion pieces.

VARIATIONS
This is a versatile recipe and is ideal for using up leftovers. Use cooked chicken or turkey instead of the ham, doubling the quantity if you omit the prawns.

3 Heat about half the oil in a wok, stir-fry the peas, prawns and ham for 1 minute, then add the soy sauce and rice wine or sherry. Transfer to a bowl and keep hot.

4 Heat the remaining oil in the wok and scramble the eggs lightly. Add the rice and stir to make sure that the grains are separate. Add the remaining salt, the remaining spring onions and the prawn mixture. Toss over the heat to mix. Serve hot or cold.

CHICKEN AND BASIL COCONUT RICE

FOR THIS DISH, THE RICE IS PARTIALLY BOILED BEFORE BEING SIMMERED WITH COCONUT SO THAT IT FULLY ABSORBS THE FLAVOUR OF THE CHILLIES, BASIL AND SPICES.

SERVES FOUR

INGREDIENTS
  350g/12oz/1¾ cups Thai fragrant
    rice, rinsed
  30–45ml/2–3 tbsp groundnut oil
  1 large onion, finely sliced into rings
  1 garlic clove, crushed
  1 fresh red chilli, seeded and finely
    sliced
  1 fresh green chilli, seeded and
    finely sliced
  generous handful of basil leaves
  3 skinless, boneless chicken breasts,
    about 350g/12oz, finely sliced
  5mm/¼in piece of lemon grass,
    pounded or finely chopped
  50g/2oz piece of creamed coconut
    dissolved in 600ml/1 pint/2½ cups
    boiling water
  salt and freshly ground black pepper

1 Bring a saucepan of lightly salted water to the boil. Add the rice to the pan and boil for about 6 minutes, until partially cooked. Drain.

2 Heat the oil in a frying pan and fry the onion rings for 5–10 minutes until golden and crisp. Lift out, drain on kitchen paper and set aside.

3 Fry the garlic and chillies in the oil remaining in the pan for 2–3 minutes, then add the basil leaves and fry briefly until they begin to wilt. Remove a few leaves and set them aside for the garnish, then add the chicken slices with the lemon grass and fry for 2–3 minutes until golden.

4 Add the rice. Stir-fry for a few minutes to coat the grains, then pour in the coconut liquid. Cook for 4–5 minutes or until the rice is tender, adding a little more water if necessary. Adjust the seasoning. Pile the rice into a warmed serving dish, scatter with the fried onion rings and basil leaves, and serve immediately.

INDONESIAN PINEAPPLE RICE

THIS WAY OF PRESENTING RICE NOT ONLY LOOKS SPECTACULAR, IT ALSO TASTES SO GOOD THAT IT CAN EASILY BE SERVED SOLO.

SERVES FOUR

INGREDIENTS
  75g/3oz/¾ cup natural peanuts
  1 large pineapple
  45ml/3 tbsp groundnut or sunflower
    oil
  1 onion, chopped
  1 garlic clove, crushed
  2 chicken breasts, about 225g/8oz,
    cut into strips
  225g/8oz/generous 1 cup Thai
    fragrant rice, rinsed
  600ml/1 pint/2½ cups chicken stock
  1 lemon grass stalk, bruised
  2 thick slices of ham, cut into
    julienne strips
  1 fresh red chilli, seeded and very
    finely sliced
  salt

1 Dry-fry the peanuts in a non-stick frying pan until golden. When cool, grind one-sixth of them in a coffee or herb mill and chop the remainder.

2 Cut a lengthways slice of pineapple, slicing through the leaves, then cut out the flesh to leave a neat shell. Chop 115g/4oz of the pineapple into cubes; saving the remainder for another dish.

3 Heat the oil in a saucepan and fry the onion and garlic for 3–4 minutes until soft. Add the chicken strips and stir-fry over a medium heat for a few minutes until evenly brown.

4 Add the rice to the pan. Toss with the chicken mixture for a few minutes, then pour in the stock, with the lemon grass and a little salt. Bring to just below boiling point, then lower the heat, cover the pan and simmer gently for 10–12 minutes until both the rice and the chicken pieces are tender.

5 Stir the chopped peanuts, the pineapple cubes and the ham into the rice, then spoon the mixture into the pineapple shell. Sprinkle the ground peanuts and the sliced chilli over the top and serve.

PERSIAN RICE WITH A TAHDEEG

*PERSIAN OR IRANIAN CUISINE IS EXOTIC AND DELICIOUS, AND THE FLAVOURS ARE INTENSE.
A TAHDEEG IS THE GLORIOUS, GOLDEN RICE CRUST OR "DIG" THAT FORMS ON THE BOTTOM OF
THE SAUCEPAN AS THE RICE COOKS.*

SERVES SIX TO EIGHT

INGREDIENTS
  450g/1lb/2⅓ cups basmati rice,
    soaked
  150ml/¼ pint/⅔ cup sunflower oil
  2 garlic cloves, crushed
  2 onions, 1 chopped, 1 finely sliced
  150g/5oz/⅔ cup green lentils, soaked
  600ml/1 pint/2½ cups stock
  50g/2oz/⅓ cup raisins
  10ml/2 tsp ground coriander
  45ml/3 tbsp tomato purée
  a few saffron strands
  1 egg yolk, beaten
  10ml/2 tsp natural yogurt
  75g/3oz/6 tbsp melted ghee or
    clarified butter
  salt and freshly ground black pepper

1 Drain the rice, then cook it in plenty
of boiling salted water for 10–12
minutes or until tender. Drain again.

2 Heat 30ml/2 tbsp of the oil in a large
saucepan and fry the garlic and the
chopped onion for 5 minutes. Stir in the
lentils, stock, raisins, ground coriander
and tomato purée, with salt and pepper
to taste. Bring to the boil, then lower
the heat, cover and simmer for about
20 minutes.

3 Soak the saffron strands in a little
hot water. Mix the egg yolk and yogurt
in a bowl. Spoon in about 120ml/4 fl oz/
½ cup of the cooked rice and mix
thoroughly. Season well.

4 Heat about two-thirds of the
remaining oil in a large saucepan.
Scatter the egg and yogurt rice evenly
over the bottom of the pan.

COOK'S TIP
In Iran, aromatic white basmati rice
would traditionally be used for this dish,
but you could use any long grain rice, or
a brown rice, if you prefer.

5 Scatter the remaining rice into the
pan, alternating it with the lentil
mixture. Build up in a pyramid shape
away from the sides of the pan,
finishing with a layer of plain rice.
With a long wooden spoon handle,
make three holes down to the bottom of
the pan; drizzle over the melted ghee or
butter. Bring to a high heat, then wrap
the pan lid in a clean, wet dish towel
and place firmly on top. When a good
head of steam appears, turn the heat
down to low. Cook slowly for about
30 minutes.

6 Meanwhile, fry the onion slices in
the remaining oil until browned and
crisp. Drain well. Remove the rice pan
from the heat, keeping it covered, and
plunge the base briefly into a sink of
cold water to loosen the rice on the
bottom. Strain the saffron water into
a bowl and stir in a few spoons of the
white rice.

7 Toss the rice and lentils together in
the pan and spoon out on to a serving
dish, mounding the mixture. Scatter
the saffron rice on top. Break up the
rice crust on the bottom of the pan
and place pieces of it around the
mound. Scatter over the crispy fried
onions and serve.

RICE <u>WITH</u> DILL <u>AND</u> BROAD BEANS

THIS IS A FAVOURITE RICE DISH IN IRAN, WHERE IT IS CALLED BAGHALI POLO. THE COMBINATION OF BROAD BEANS, DILL AND WARM SPICES WORKS VERY WELL, AND THE SAFFRON RICE ADDS A SPLASH OF BRIGHT COLOUR.

SERVES FOUR

INGREDIENTS
275g/10oz/1½ cups basmati rice,
   soaked
750ml/1¼ pints/3 cups water
40g/1½oz/3 tbsp melted butter
175g/6oz/1½ cups frozen baby broad
   beans, thawed and peeled
90ml/6 tbsp finely chopped fresh
   dill, plus 1 fresh dill sprig, to
   garnish
5ml/1 tsp ground cinnamon
5ml/1 tsp ground cumin
2–3 saffron strands, soaked in
   15ml/1 tbsp boiling water
salt

1 Drain the rice, tip it into a saucepan and pour in the water. Add a little salt. Bring to the boil, then lower the heat and simmer very gently for 5 minutes. Drain, rinse well in warm water and drain once again.

2 Melt the butter in a non-stick saucepan. Pour two-thirds of the melted butter into a small jug and set aside. Spoon enough rice into the pan to cover the bottom. Add a quarter of the beans and a little dill. Spread over another layer of rice, then a layer of beans and dill. Repeat the layers until all the beans and dill have been used up, ending with a layer of rice. Cook over a gentle heat for 8 minutes until nearly tender.

3 Pour the reserved melted butter over the rice. Sprinkle with the ground cinnamon and cumin. Cover the pan with a clean dish towel and a tight-fitting lid, lifting the corners of the cloth back over the lid. Cook over a low heat for 25–30 minutes.

4 Spoon about 45ml/3 tbsp of the cooked rice into the bowl of saffron water; mix well. Mound the remaining rice mixture on a large serving plate and spoon the saffron rice on one side to decorate. Serve at once, decorated with the sprig of dill.

ALMA-ATA

THIS DISH COMES FROM CENTRAL ASIA AND IS A SPECTACULAR COMBINATION OF THE FRUITS AND NUTS FROM THAT REGION.

SERVES FOUR

INGREDIENTS

  75g/3oz/¾ cup blanched almonds
  60ml/4 tbsp sunflower oil
  225g/8oz carrots, cut into julienne
    strips
  2 onions, chopped
  115g/4oz/½ cup ready-to-eat dried
    apricots, chopped
  50g/2oz/⅓ cup raisins
  350g/12oz/1¾ cups basmati rice,
    soaked
  600ml/1 pint/2½ cups vegetable stock
  150ml/¼ pint/⅔ cup orange juice
  grated rind of 1 orange
  25g/1oz/⅓ cup pine nuts
  1 red eating apple, chopped
  salt and freshly ground black pepper

3 Pour in the vegetable stock and orange juice, stirring constantly, then stir in the orange rind. Reserve a few toasted almonds for the garnish and stir in the remainder with the pine nuts. Cover the pan with a double piece of foil and fit the casserole lid securely. Transfer to the oven and bake for 30–35 minutes, until the rice is tender and all the liquid has been absorbed.

4 Remove from the oven, season to taste and stir in the chopped apple. Serve from the casserole or spoon into a warmed serving dish. Garnish with the reserved almonds.

1 Preheat the oven to 160°C/325°F/ Gas 3. Toast the almonds in a dry frying pan for 4–5 minutes until golden.

2 Heat the oil in a heavy, flameproof casserole and fry the carrots and onions over a moderately high heat for 6–8 minutes until both are slightly glazed. Add the apricots, raisins and rice and cook over a medium heat for a few minutes, stirring all the time, until the grains of rice are coated in the oil.

VARIATION

For a one-dish meal, add 450g/1lb lamb, cut into cubes. Brown in the casserole in a little oil, then transfer to a dish while you cook the onion and carrots. Stir the meat back into the casserole when you add the stock and orange juice.

CELEBRATION PAELLA

THIS PAELLA IS A MARVELLOUS MIXTURE OF SOME OF THE FINEST SPANISH INGREDIENTS. CHICKEN AND RABBIT, SEAFOOD AND VEGETABLES ARE MIXED WITH RICE TO MAKE A COLOURFUL PARTY DISH.

SERVES SIX TO EIGHT

INGREDIENTS
    450g/1lb fresh mussels
    90ml/6 tbsp white wine
    150g/5oz French beans, cut into
        2.5cm/1in lengths
    115g/4oz/1 cup frozen broad beans
    6 small skinless, boneless chicken
        breasts, cut into large pieces
    30ml/2 tbsp plain flour, seasoned
        with salt and pepper
    about 90ml/6 tbsp olive oil
    6–8 large raw prawns, tailed and
        deveined, or 12 smaller raw prawns
    150g/5oz pork fillet, cut into bite-
        size pieces
    2 onions, chopped
    2–3 garlic cloves, crushed
    1 red pepper, seeded and sliced
    2 ripe tomatoes, peeled, seeded and
        chopped
    900ml/1½ pints/3¾ cups well-
        flavoured chicken stock
    good pinch of saffron, dissolved in
        30ml/2 tbsp hot water
    350g/12oz/1¾ cups Spanish rice or
        risotto rice
    225g/8oz chorizo sausage, thickly
        sliced
    115g/4oz/1 cup frozen peas
    6–8 stuffed green olives, thickly
        sliced

COOK'S TIP
Ideally, you need to use a paella pan
for this dish and, strictly speaking, the
paella shouldn't be stirred during
cooking. You may find, though, that –
because of the distribution of heat – the
rice cooks in the centre but not around
the outside. (This doesn't happen if
paella is cooked traditionally – outdoors,
on a large wood fire.) To make sure your
paella cooks evenly, you could break the
rule and stir occasionally, or cook the
paella on the sole of a hot 190°C/375°F/
Gas 5 oven for about 15–18 minutes.
The result should be practically identical,
but in Spain this would be termed an
arroz – a rice – rather than paella.

1 Scrub the mussels, discarding any
that do not close when sharply tapped.
Place in a large saucepan with the
wine, bring to the boil, then cover the
pan tightly and cook for 3–4 minutes
until all the mussels have opened,
shaking the pan occasionally. Drain,
reserving the liquid and discarding any
mussels that have not opened.

2 Briefly cook the green beans and
broad beans in separate pans of boiling
water for 2–3 minutes. Drain. As soon
as the broad beans are cool enough to
handle, pop them out of their skins.

3 Dust the chicken with the seasoned
flour. Heat half the oil in a paella pan or
deep frying pan and fry the chicken
until evenly browned. Transfer to a
plate. Fry the prawns briefly, adding
more oil if needed, then use a slotted
spoon to transfer them to a plate. Heat
a further 30ml/2 tbsp of the oil in the
pan and brown the pork evenly.
Transfer to a separate plate.

4 Heat the remaining oil and fry the
onions and garlic for 3–4 minutes until
golden brown. Add the red pepper,
cook for 2–3 minutes, then add the
chopped tomatoes and cook until the
mixture is fairly thick.

5 Stir in the chicken stock, the
reserved mussel liquid and the saffron
liquid. Season well with salt and pepper
and bring to the boil. When the liquid is
bubbling, throw in all the rice. Stir once,
then add the chicken pieces, pork,
prawns, beans, chorizo and peas. Cook
over a moderately high heat for 12
minutes, then lower the heat and leave
to cook for 8–10 minutes more, until all
the liquid has been absorbed.

6 Add the mussels and olives and
continue cooking for a further 3–4
minutes to heat through. Remove the
pan from the heat, cover with a clean
damp dish towel and leave to stand for
10 minutes before serving from the pan.

PERUVIAN DUCK WITH RICE

THIS IS A VERY RICH DISH, BRIGHTLY COLOURED WITH SPANISH TOMATOES AND FRESH HERBS.

SERVES FOUR TO SIX

INGREDIENTS
    4 boned duck breasts
    1 Spanish onion, chopped
    2 garlic cloves, crushed
    10ml/2 tsp grated fresh root ginger
    4 tomatoes (peeled, if liked),
        chopped
    225g/8oz Kabocha or onion squash,
        cut into 1cm/½in cubes
    275g/10oz/1½ cups long grain rice
    750ml/1¼ pints/3 cups chicken
        stock
    15ml/1 tbsp finely chopped fresh
        coriander
    15ml/1 tbsp finely chopped fresh
        mint
    salt and freshly ground black
        pepper

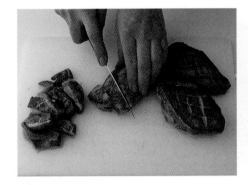

2 Pour all but 15ml/1 tbsp of the fat into a jar or cup, then fry the breasts, meat side down, in the fat remaining in the pan for 3–4 minutes until brown all over. Transfer to a board, slice thickly and set aside in a shallow dish. Deglaze the pan with a little water and pour this liquid over the duck.

4 Add the squash, stir-fry for a few minutes, then cover and allow to steam for about 4 minutes.

1 Heat a heavy-based frying pan or flameproof casserole. Using a sharp knife, score the fatty side of the duck breasts in a criss-cross pattern, rub the fat with a little salt, then dry-fry the duck, skin side down, for 6–8 minutes to render some of the fat.

3 Fry the onion and garlic in the same pan for 4–5 minutes until the onion is fairly soft, adding a little extra duck fat if necessary. Stir in the ginger, cook for 1–2 minutes more, then add the tomatoes and cook, stirring, for another 2 minutes.

5 Stir in the rice and cook, stirring, until the rice is coated in the tomato and onion mixture. Pour in the stock, return the slices of duck to the pan and season with salt and pepper.

6 Bring to the boil, then lower the heat, cover and simmer gently for 30–35 minutes until the rice is tender. Stir in the coriander and mint and serve.

COOK'S TIP
While rice was originally imported to South America, squash was very much an indigenous vegetable. Pumpkin could also be used for this recipe. Kabocha squash has a thick skin and lots of seeds, which need to be removed before the flesh is cubed.

VARIATION
In Peru, these kinds of all-in-one dishes are based around whatever meat is available in the shops, or, in the case of vegetables, what is growing in the garden. Chicken or rabbit can be used instead of duck, and courgettes and carrots would work well when squash is out of season.

LOUISIANA RICE

AUBERGINE AND PORK COMBINE WITH HERBS AND SPICES TO MAKE A HIGHLY FLAVOURSOME DISH.

SERVES FOUR

INGREDIENTS
  60ml/4 tbsp vegetable oil
  1 onion, chopped
  1 small aubergine, diced
  225g/8oz minced pork
  1 green pepper, seeded and
    chopped
  2 celery sticks, chopped
  1 garlic clove, crushed
  5ml/1 tsp cayenne pepper
  5ml/1 tsp paprika
  5ml/1 tsp freshly ground black
    pepper
  2.5ml/½ tsp salt
  5ml/1 tsp dried thyme
  2.5ml/½ tsp dried oregano
  475ml/16fl oz/2 cups chicken stock
  225g/8oz chicken livers, chopped
  150g/5oz/¾ cup white long grain rice
  1 bay leaf
  45ml/3 tbsp chopped fresh parsley

1 Heat the oil in a frying pan. When it is piping hot, add the onion and aubergine and stir-fry for about 5 minutes.

2 Add the pork and cook for 6–8 minutes until browned, using a wooden spoon to break up any lumps.

3 Stir in the green pepper, celery and garlic, with all the spices and herbs. Cover and cook over a high heat for 9–10 minutes, stirring frequently from the bottom of the pan to scrape up and distribute the crispy brown bits.

4 Pour in the chicken stock and stir to remove any sediment from the bottom of the pan. Cover and cook for 6 minutes over a moderate heat. Stir in the chicken livers and cook for 2 minutes more.

5 Stir in the rice and add the bay leaf. Lower the heat, cover and simmer for 6–7 minutes. Turn off the heat and leave to stand, still covered, for 10–15 minutes more until the rice is tender. Remove the bay leaf and stir in the chopped parsley. Serve the rice hot.

SALMON AND RICE GRATIN

THIS ALL-IN-ONE SUPPER DISH IS IDEAL FOR INFORMAL ENTERTAINING AS IT CAN BE MADE AHEAD OF TIME AND REHEATED FOR ABOUT HALF AN HOUR BEFORE BEING SERVED WITH A TOSSED SALAD.

SERVES SIX

INGREDIENTS
  675g/1½lb fresh salmon fillet,
    skinned
  1 bay leaf
  a few parsley stalks
  1 litre/1¾ pints/4 cups water
  400g/14oz/2 cups basmati rice,
    soaked and drained
  30–45ml/2–3 tbsp chopped fresh
    parsley, plus extra to garnish
  175g/6oz/1½ cups Cheddar cheese,
    grated
  3 hard-boiled eggs, chopped
  salt and freshly ground black pepper
For the sauce
  1 litre/1¾ pints/4 cups milk
  40g/1½oz/⅓ cup plain flour
  40g/1½oz/3 tbsp butter
  5ml/1 tsp mild curry paste or French
    mustard

1 Put the salmon in a wide, shallow pan. Add the bay leaf and parsley stalks, with salt and pepper. Pour in the water and bring to simmering point. Poach the fish for about 12 minutes until just tender.

2 Lift the fish out of the pan using a slotted spoon, then strain the liquid into a saucepan. Leave the fish to cool, then remove any visible bones and flake the flesh gently with a fork.

3 Drain the rice and add it to the saucepan containing the fish-poaching liquid. Bring to the boil, then lower the heat, cover and simmer for 10 minutes without lifting the lid.

4 Remove the pan from the heat and, without lifting the lid, allow the rice to stand undisturbed for 5 minutes.

5 Meanwhile, make the sauce. Mix the milk, flour and butter in a saucepan. Bring to the boil over a low heat, whisking constantly until the sauce is smooth and thick. Stir in the curry paste or mustard, with salt and pepper to taste. Simmer for 2 minutes.

6 Preheat the grill. Remove the sauce from the heat and stir in the chopped parsley and rice, with half the cheese. Using a large metal spoon, fold in the flaked fish and eggs. Spoon into a shallow gratin dish and sprinkle with the rest of the cheese. Heat under the grill until the topping is golden brown and bubbling. Serve in individual dishes, garnished with chopped parsley.

VARIATIONS
Prawns could be substituted for the salmon, and other hard cheeses, such as Lancashire or Red Leicester, could be used instead of the Cheddar.

CHICKEN AND PRAWN JAMBALAYA

THE MIXTURE OF CHICKEN, SEAFOOD AND RICE SUGGESTS A CLOSE RELATIONSHIP TO THE SPANISH PAELLA, BUT THE NAME IS MORE LIKELY TO HAVE DERIVED FROM JAMBON (THE FRENCH FOR HAM), À LA YA (CREOLE FOR RICE). JAMBALAYAS ARE A COLOURFUL MIXTURE OF HIGHLY FLAVOURED INGREDIENTS, AND ARE ALWAYS MADE IN LARGE QUANTITIES FOR FEASTS AND CELEBRATION MEALS.

SERVES TEN

INGREDIENTS

    2 chickens, each about 1.5kg/3–3½lb
    450g/1lb piece raw smoked gammon
    50g/2oz/4 tbsp lard or bacon fat
    50g/2oz/½ cup plain flour
    3 medium onions, finely sliced
    2 green peppers, seeded and sliced
    675g/1½lb tomatoes, peeled and
      chopped
    2–3 garlic cloves, crushed
    10ml/2 tsp chopped fresh thyme or
      5ml/1 tsp dried thyme
    24 raw Mediterranean prawns, peeled
      and deveined
    500g/1¼lb/3 cups white long grain rice
    1.2 litres/2 pints/5 cups water
    2–3 dashes Tabasco sauce
    45ml/3 tbsp chopped fresh flat leaf
      parsley, plus tiny fresh parsley
      sprigs, to garnish
    salt and freshly ground black pepper

1 Cut each chicken into 10 pieces and season with salt and pepper. Dice the gammon, discarding the rind and fat.

2 Melt the lard or bacon fat in a large, heavy-based frying pan. Add the chicken pieces in batches, brown them all over, then lift them out with a slotted spoon and set them aside.

3 Reduce the heat. Sprinkle the flour into the fat in the pan and stir until the roux turns golden brown. Return the chicken pieces to the pan.

4 Add the diced gammon, onions, green peppers, tomatoes, garlic and thyme. Cook, stirring regularly, for 10 minutes, then add the prawns and mix lightly.

5 Stir the rice into the pan and pour in the water. Season with salt, pepper and Tabasco sauce. Bring to the boil, then cook gently until the rice is tender and all the liquid has been absorbed. Add a little extra boiling water if the rice looks like drying out before it is cooked.

6 Mix the parsley into the finished dish, garnish with tiny sprigs of flat leaf parsley and serve immediately.

PROVENÇAL RICE

ONE OF THE GLORIOUS THINGS ABOUT FOOD FROM THE SOUTH OF FRANCE IS ITS COLOUR, AND THIS DISH IS NO EXCEPTION. TO SERVE AS A MAIN COURSE, ALLOW 50G/2OZ/¼ CUP RICE PER PERSON.

SERVES FOUR

INGREDIENTS

2 onions
90ml/6 tbsp olive oil
175g/6oz/scant 1 cup brown long
  grain rice
10ml/2 tsp mustard seeds
475ml/16fl oz/2 cups vegetable stock
1 large or 2 small red peppers,
  seeded and cut into chunks
1 small aubergine, cut into cubes
2–3 courgettes, sliced
about 12 cherry tomatoes
5–6 fresh basil leaves, torn into
  pieces
2 garlic cloves, finely chopped
60ml/4 tbsp white wine
60ml/4 tbsp passata or tomato
  juice
2 hard-boiled eggs, cut into wedges
8 stuffed green olives, sliced
15ml/1 tbsp capers
3 drained sun-dried tomatoes in oil,
  sliced (optional)
butter
sea salt and freshly ground black
  pepper

1 Preheat the oven to 200°C/400°F/ Gas 6. Finely chop one onion. Heat 30ml/2 tbsp of the oil in a saucepan and fry the chopped onion over a gentle heat for 5–6 minutes until softened.

2 Add the rice and mustard seeds. Cook, stirring, for 2 minutes, then add the stock and a little salt. Bring to the boil, then lower the heat, cover and simmer for 35 minutes until the rice is tender.

3 Meanwhile, cut the remaining onion into wedges. Put these in a roasting tin with the peppers, aubergine, courgettes and cherry tomatoes. Scatter over the torn basil leaves and chopped garlic. Pour over the remaining olive oil and sprinkle with sea salt and black pepper. Roast for 15–20 minutes until the vegetables begin to char, stirring halfway through cooking. Reduce the oven temperature to 180°C/350°F/Gas 4.

4 Spoon the rice into an earthenware casserole. Put the roasted vegetables on top, together with any vegetable juices from the roasting tin, then pour over the wine and passata.

5 Arrange the egg wedges on top of the vegetables, with the sliced olives, capers and sun-dried tomatoes, if using. Dot with butter, cover and cook for 15–20 minutes until heated through.

RED RICE AND ROASTED RED PEPPER SALAD

PEPPERS, SUN-DRIED TOMATOES AND GARLIC GIVE A DISTINCTLY MEDITERRANEAN FLAVOUR TO THIS SALAD DISH. IT MAKES AN EXCELLENT ACCOMPANIMENT TO SPICY SAUSAGES OR FISH.

SERVES FOUR

INGREDIENTS

225g/8oz/generous 1 cup Camargue red rice
vegetable or chicken stock or water (see method)
45ml/3 tbsp olive oil
3 red peppers, seeded and sliced into strips
4–5 sun-dried tomatoes
4–5 whole garlic cloves, unpeeled
1 onion, chopped
30ml/2 tbsp chopped fresh parsley, plus extra to garnish
15ml/1 tbsp chopped fresh coriander
10ml/2 tsp balsamic vinegar
salt and freshly ground black pepper

1 Cook the rice in stock or water, following instructions on the packet. Heat the oil in a frying pan and add the peppers. Cook over a medium heat for 4 minutes, shaking occasionally.

2 Lower the heat, add the sun-dried tomatoes, whole garlic cloves and onion, cover the pan and cook for 8–10 minutes more, stirring occasionally. Remove the lid and cook for 3 minutes more.

3 Off the heat, stir in the parsley, coriander and vinegar, and season. Spread the rice out on a serving dish and spoon the pepper mixture on top. Peel the whole garlic cloves, cut the flesh into slices and scatter these over the salad. Serve at room temperature, garnished with more fresh parsley.

CREAMY FISH PILAU

THIS DISH IS INSPIRED BY A FUSION OF CUISINES – THE METHOD COMES FROM INDIA AND USES THAT COUNTRY'S FAVOURITE RICE, BASMATI, BUT THE DELICIOUS WINE AND CREAM SAUCE IS VERY MUCH FRENCH IN FLAVOUR.

SERVES FOUR TO SIX

INGREDIENTS

450g/1lb fresh mussels, scrubbed
350ml/12fl oz/1½ cups white wine
fresh parsley sprig
about 675g/1½lb salmon
225g/8oz scallops
about 15ml/1 tbsp olive oil
40g/1½oz/3 tbsp butter
2 shallots, finely chopped
225g/8oz/3 cups button mushrooms, halved if large
275g/10oz/1½ cups basmati rice, soaked
300ml/½ pint/1¼ cups fish stock
150ml/¼ pint/⅔ cup double cream
15ml/1 tbsp chopped fresh parsley
225g/8oz large cooked prawns, peeled and deveined
salt and freshly ground black pepper
fresh flat leaf parsley sprigs, to garnish

1 Preheat the oven to 160°C/325°F/ Gas 3. Place the mussels in a pan with 90ml/6 tbsp of the wine and parsley, cover and cook for 4–5 minutes until they have opened. Drain, reserving the cooking liquid. Remove the mussels from their shells, discarding any that have not opened.

2 Cut the fish into bite-size pieces. Detach the corals from the scallops and cut the white scallop flesh into thick pieces.

3 Heat half the olive oil and butter and fry the shallots and mushrooms for 3–4 minutes. Transfer to a large bowl. Heat the remaining oil in the frying pan and fry the rice for 2–3 minutes, stirring until it is coated in oil. Spoon the rice into a deep casserole.

4 Pour the stock, remaining wine and reserved mussel liquid into the frying pan, and bring to the boil. Off the heat, stir in the cream and parsley; season lightly. Pour over the rice and then add the salmon and the scallop flesh, together with the mushroom mixture. Stir carefully to mix.

5 Cover the casserole tightly. Bake for 30–35 minutes, then add the corals, replace the cover and cook for 4 minutes more. Add the mussels and prawns, cover and cook for 3–4 minutes until the seafood is heated through and the rice is tender. Serve garnished with the parsley sprigs.

AFRICAN LAMB AND VEGETABLE PILAU

Spicy lamb is served in this dish with basmati rice and a colourful selection of different vegetables and cashew nuts. Lamb and rice are a popular combination in African cooking.

SERVES FOUR

INGREDIENTS
450g/1lb boned shoulder of lamb, cubed
2.5ml/½ tsp dried thyme
2.5ml/½ tsp paprika
5ml/1 tsp garam masala
1 garlic clove, crushed
25ml/1½ tbsp vegetable oil
900ml/1½ pints/3¾ cups lamb stock
savoy cabbage or crisp lettuce leaves, to serve

For the rice
25g/1oz/2 tbsp butter
1 onion, chopped
1 medium potato, diced
1 carrot, sliced
½ red pepper, seeded and chopped
1 fresh green chilli, seeded and chopped
115g/4oz/1 cup sliced green cabbage
60ml/4 tbsp natural yogurt
2.5ml/½ tsp ground cumin
5 green cardamom pods
2 garlic cloves, crushed
225g/8oz/generous 1 cup basmati rice, soaked
about 50g/2oz/½ cup cashew nuts
salt and freshly ground black pepper

1 Put the lamb cubes in a large bowl and add the thyme, paprika, garam masala and garlic, with plenty of salt and pepper. Stir, cover, and leave in a cool place for 2–3 hours.

2 Heat the oil in a saucepan and fry the lamb, in batches if necessary, over a medium heat for 5–6 minutes, until browned. Stir in the stock, cover the pan and cook for 35–40 minutes. Using a slotted spoon, transfer the lamb to a bowl. Pour the liquid into a measuring jug, topping it up with water if necessary to make 600ml/1 pint/2½ cups.

COOK'S TIP
If the stock looks a bit fatty after cooking the lamb cubes, blot the surface with kitchen paper to remove the excess grease before pouring the stock into the measuring jug.

3 Melt the butter in a separate pan and fry the onion, potato and carrot for 5 minutes. Add the red pepper and chilli and fry for 3 minutes more, then stir in the cabbage, yogurt, spices, garlic and the reserved lamb stock. Stir well, cover, then simmer gently for 5–10 minutes, until the cabbage has wilted.

4 Drain the rice and stir into the stew with the lamb. Cover and simmer over a low heat for 20 minutes or until the rice is cooked. Sprinkle in the cashew nuts and season to taste with salt and pepper. Serve hot, cupped in cabbage or lettuce leaves.

WILD RICE PILAFF

WILD RICE ISN'T A RICE AT ALL, BUT IS ACTUALLY A TYPE OF WILD GRASS. CALL IT WHAT YOU WILL, IT HAS A WONDERFUL NUTTY FLAVOUR AND COMBINES WELL WITH LONG GRAIN RICE IN THIS FRUITY MIXTURE. SERVE AS A SIDE DISH.

SERVES SIX

INGREDIENTS
  200g/7oz/1 cup wild rice
  40g/1½oz/3 tbsp butter
  ½ onion, finely chopped
  200g/7oz/1 cup long grain rice
  475ml/16fl oz/2 cups chicken stock
  75g/3oz/¾ cup sliced or flaked
    almonds
  115g/4oz/⅔ cup sultanas
  30ml/2 tbsp chopped fresh parsley
  salt and freshly ground black pepper

1 Bring a large saucepan of water to the boil. Add the wild rice and 5ml/ 1 tsp salt. Lower the heat, cover and simmer gently for 45–60 minutes, until the rice is tender. Drain well.

2 Meanwhile, melt 15g/½oz/1 tbsp of the butter in another saucepan. Add the onion and cook over a medium heat for about 5 minutes until it is just softened. Stir in the long grain rice and cook for 1 minute more.

3 Stir in the stock and bring to the boil. Cover and simmer gently for 30–40 minutes, until the rice is tender and the liquid has been absorbed.

COOK'S TIP
Like all rice dishes, this one must be made with well-flavoured stock. If you haven't time to make your own, use a carton or can of good quality stock.

4 Melt the remaining butter in a small pan. Add the almonds and cook until they are just golden. Set aside.

5 Put the rice mixture in a bowl and add the almonds, sultanas and half the parsley. Stir to mix. Taste and adjust the seasoning if necessary. Transfer to a warmed serving dish, sprinkle with the remaining parsley and serve.

MOROCCAN PAELLA

PAELLA IS PERENNIALLY POPULAR. THIS VERSION HAS CROSSED THE SEA FROM SPAIN TO MOROCCO, AND ACQUIRED SOME SPICY TOUCHES. UNLIKE SPANISH PAELLA, IT IS MADE WITH LONG GRAIN RICE.

SERVES SIX

INGREDIENTS

2 large skinless, boneless chicken breasts
about 150g/5oz prepared squid, cut into rings
275g/10oz cod or haddock fillets, skinned and cut into bite-size chunks
8–10 raw king prawns, peeled and deveined
8 scallops, trimmed and halved
350g/12oz fresh mussels
250g/9oz/1⅓ cups white long grain rice
30ml/2 tbsp sunflower oil
1 bunch spring onions, cut into strips
2 small courgettes, cut into strips
1 red pepper, cored, seeded and cut into strips
400ml/14fl oz/1⅔ cups chicken stock
250ml/8fl oz/1 cup passata
salt and freshly ground black pepper
fresh coriander sprigs and lemon wedges, to garnish

For the marinade

2 fresh red chillies, seeded and roughly chopped
generous handful of fresh coriander
10–15ml/2–3 tsp ground cumin
15ml/1 tbsp paprika
2 garlic cloves
45ml/3 tbsp olive oil
60ml/4 tbsp sunflower oil
juice of 1 lemon

1 Make the marinade. Place all the ingredients in a food processor with 5ml/1 tsp salt and process until thoroughly blended. Cut the chicken into bite-size pieces. Place in a bowl.

2 Place the fish and shellfish (apart from the mussels) in a separate glass bowl. Divide the marinade between the fish and chicken and stir well. Cover with clear film and leave to marinate for at least 2 hours.

3 Scrub the mussels, discarding any that do not close when tapped sharply, and keep in a bowl in the fridge until ready to use. Place the rice in a bowl, cover with boiling water and set aside for about 30 minutes. Drain the chicken and fish, and reserve both lots of the marinade. Heat the oil in a wok, balti pan or paella pan and fry the chicken pieces for a few minutes until lightly browned.

4 Add the spring onions to the pan, fry for 1 minute and then add the courgettes and red pepper and fry for 3–4 minutes more until slightly softened. Transfer the chicken and then the vegetables to separate plates.

5 Scrape all the marinade into the pan and cook for 1 minute. Drain the rice, add to the pan and cook for 1 minute. Add the chicken stock, passata and reserved chicken, season with salt and pepper and stir well. Bring the mixture to the boil, then cover the pan with a large lid or foil and simmer very gently for 10–15 minutes until the rice is almost tender.

6 Add the reserved vegetables to the pan and place all the fish and mussels on top. Cover again with a lid or foil and cook over a moderate heat for 10–12 minutes until the fish is cooked and the mussels have opened. Discard any mussels that remain closed. Serve garnished with fresh coriander and lemon wedges.

CARIBBEAN CHICKEN WITH PIGEON PEA RICE

GOLDEN, SPICY CARAMELIZED CHICKEN TOPS A RICHLY FLAVOURED VEGETABLE RICE IN THIS HEARTY AND DELICIOUS SUPPER DISH. PIGEON PEAS ARE A COMMON INGREDIENT IN CARIBBEAN COOKING.

SERVES FOUR

INGREDIENTS
  5ml/1 tsp allspice
  2.5ml/½ tsp ground cinnamon
  5ml/1 tsp dried thyme
  pinch of ground cloves
  1.5ml/¼ tsp freshly grated nutmeg
  4 skinless, boneless chicken breasts
  45ml/3 tbsp groundnut or sunflower
    oil
  15g/½oz/1 tbsp butter
  1 onion, chopped
  2 garlic cloves, crushed
  1 carrot, diced
  1 celery stick, chopped
  3 spring onions, chopped
  1 fresh red chilli, seeded and thinly
    sliced
  400g/14oz can pigeon peas
  225g/8oz/generous 1 cup long grain
    rice
  120ml/4fl oz/½ cup coconut milk
  550ml/18fl oz/2½ cups chicken
    stock
  30ml/2 tbsp demerara sugar
  salt and cayenne pepper

1 Mix together the allspice, cinnamon, thyme, cloves and nutmeg. Rub the mixture all over the pieces of chicken. Set aside for 30 minutes.

2 Heat 15ml/1 tbsp of the oil with the butter in a saucepan. Fry the onion and garlic over a medium heat until soft and beginning to brown. Add the carrot, celery, spring onions and chilli. Sauté for a few minutes, then stir in the pigeon peas, rice, coconut milk and chicken stock. Season with salt and cayenne pepper. Bring to simmering point, cover and cook over a low heat for about 25 minutes.

COOK'S TIP
Pigeon peas are sometimes called gungo beans, especially when sold in ethnic markets. If they are not available, use borlotti beans instead.

3 About 10 minutes before the rice mixture is cooked, heat the remaining oil in a heavy-based frying pan, add the sugar and cook, without stirring, until it begins to caramelize.

4 Carefully add the chicken to the pan. Cook for 8–10 minutes until the chicken has a browned, glazed appearance and is cooked through. Transfer the chicken to a board and slice it thickly. Serve the pigeon pea rice in individual bowls, with the chicken on top.

TANZANIAN VEGETABLE RICE

SERVE THIS TASTY DISH WITH BAKED CHICKEN OR FISH. ADD THE VEGETABLES NEAR THE END OF COOKING SO THAT THEY REMAIN CRISP.

SERVES FOUR

INGREDIENTS

350g/12oz/1¾ cups basmati rice
45ml/3 tbsp vegetable oil
1 onion, chopped
2 garlic cloves, crushed
750ml/1¼ pints/3 cups vegetable
  stock or water
115g/4oz/⅔ cup fresh or drained
  canned sweetcorn kernels
½ red or green pepper, seeded and
  chopped
1 large carrot, grated
fresh chervil sprigs, to garnish

1 Rinse the rice in a sieve under cold water, then leave to drain thoroughly for about 15 minutes.

2 Heat the oil in a large saucepan and fry the onion for a few minutes over a medium heat until it starts to soften.

3 Add the rice and fry for about 10 minutes, stirring constantly to prevent the rice sticking to the pan. Then stir in the crushed garlic.

4 Pour in the stock or water and stir well. Bring to the boil, then lower the heat, cover and simmer for 10 minutes.

5 Scatter the sweetcorn kernels over the rice, then spread the chopped pepper on top. Sprinkle over the grated carrot. Cover the saucepan tightly. Steam over a low heat until the rice is tender, then mix together with a fork, pile on to a platter and garnish with chervil. Serve immediately.

CARIBBEAN PEANUT CHICKEN

PEANUT BUTTER IS USED A LOT IN MANY CARIBBEAN DISHES. IT ADDS A RICHNESS, AS WELL AS A DELICIOUS DEPTH OF FLAVOUR ALL OF ITS OWN.

SERVES FOUR

INGREDIENTS

   4 skinless, boneless chicken breasts, cut into thin strips
   225g/8oz/generous 1 cup white long grain rice
   30ml/2 tbsp groundnut oil
   15g/½oz/1 tbsp butter, plus extra for greasing
   1 onion, finely chopped
   2 tomatoes, peeled, seeded and chopped
   1 fresh green chilli, seeded and sliced
   60ml/4 tbsp smooth peanut butter
   450ml/¾ pint/scant 2 cups chicken stock
   lemon juice, to taste
   salt and freshly ground black pepper
   lime wedges and sprigs of fresh flat leaf parsley, to garnish
For the marinade
   15ml/1 tbsp sunflower oil
   1–2 garlic cloves, crushed
   5ml/1 tsp chopped fresh thyme
   25ml/1½ tbsp medium curry powder
   juice of half a lemon

1 Mix all the marinade ingredients in a large bowl and stir in the chicken. Cover loosely with clear film and set aside in a cool place for 2–3 hours.

2 Meanwhile, cook the rice in plenty of lightly salted boiling water until tender. Drain well and turn into a generously buttered casserole.

3 Preheat the oven to 180°C/350°F/Gas 4. Heat 15ml/1 tbsp of the oil and butter in a flameproof casserole and fry the chicken pieces for 4–5 minutes until evenly brown. Add more oil if necessary.

4 Transfer the chicken to a plate. Add the onion to the casserole and fry for 5–6 minutes until lightly browned, adding more oil if necessary. Stir in the chopped tomatoes and chilli. Cook over a gentle heat for 3–4 minutes, stirring occasionally. Remove from the heat.

5 Mix the peanut butter with the chicken stock. Stir into the tomato and onion mixture, then add the chicken. Stir in the lemon juice, season to taste, then spoon the mixture over the rice in the casserole.

6 Cover the casserole. Cook in the oven for 15–20 minutes or until piping hot. Use a large spoon to toss the rice with the chicken mixture. Serve at once, garnished with the lime wedges and parsley sprigs.

COOK'S TIP
If the casserole is not large enough to allow you to toss the rice with the chicken mixture before serving, invert a large, deep plate over the casserole, turn both over and toss the mixture on the plate.

INDEX